PIERO AND GLORIA CICIONESI

AUROVILLE ARCHITECTS MONOGRAPH SERIES

PIERO AND GLORIA CICIONESI

MONA DOCTOR-PINGEL

With contributions from

Poonam Verma Mascarenhas
Niharika Sanyal
and
Dr Chamanlal Gupta
Poppo Pingel
Pino Marchese

MAPIN PUBLISHING

Enjoy videos from this book on your smartphone using the free **BooksPlus** app

Scan this QR code to download the app or visit www.booksplusapp.com

How to use the app

1. Download the **BooksPlus : Augmented Reality** app.
2. Launch the app.
3. Now, point your smartphone at an image in this book with the [camera icon] symbol.
4. Enjoy the videos on pages 16-17, 39 left, 59, 65 below, 85, 92 left and 111.

   In these videos Piero and Gloria share the story of their journey and work in Auroville: Gloria recounts her first meeting with Piero, their days in Finland, arrival in Auroville and the experience of meeting The Mother. Gloria also recounts their work on the Aspiration huts and Auroson's Home in Auroville. Readers are taken through the years of construction of the Matrimandir—from The Mother's vision of it to its completion—as Alan Lithman and Piero recount the work through the various phases, including the concreting at night; lifting of the columns; marble laying on the walls, the heliostat as well as the final top ring.

BooksPlus: Augmented Reality
Powered by ignitesol.com

For further support, write to us at support@booksplusapp.com

First published in India in 2018 by
Mapin Publishing Pvt. Ltd
706 Kaivanna, Panchvati, Ellisbridge
Ahmedabad 380006 INDIA
T: +91 79 40 228 228 • F: +91 79 40 228 201
E: mapin@mapinpub.com • www.mapinpub.com

International Distribution
Worldwide (except North America and South Asia)
Prestel Publishing Ltd.
14-17 Wells Street
London W1T 3PD
T: +44 (0)20 7323 5004 • F: +44 (0)20 7323 0271
E: sales@prestel-uk.co.uk

North America
Antique Collectors' Club
T: +1 800 252 5231 • F: +1 413 529 0862
E: sales@antiquecc.com • www.accdistribution.com/us

South Asia
Mapin Publishing Pvt. Ltd

We would like to acknowledge support from Mrs Vanlila Ramakant Doctor towards enabling augmented reality videos for this book.

ISBN: 978-93-85360-41-1

Copyediting: Ateendriya Gupta / Mapin Editorial
Design: Sarayu Narasimhan and Gopal Limbad/ Mapin Design Studio
Printed at Parksons Graphics, Mumbai

CAPTIONS

FRONT COVER Future School, Auroville, 1999
BACK COVER Matrimandir space frame, Auroville, 1987
PAGE 2 Sketch of Piazza Navona in Italy, ink and watercolour, by Piero Cicionesi, 1958

This book is dedicated to all the people who made Matrimandir a Reality from a Dream.

Symbol of Auroville: The dot at the center represents Unity, the Supreme; the inner circle represents the creation, the conception of the City; the petals represent the power of expression, realization.
—The Mother, 16 August 1971

Ink sketch of the Turin countryside, Italy,
by Piero Cicionesi, 1965

Contents

Watercolour paintings on handmade paper, Piero Cicionesi, 1987

AUTHOR'S NOTE

Auroville is conceived as an urban experiment to undertake the work of "evolution of consciousness" in a society that would concretely experiment with the challenges of economy, sociology, environment and culture while seeking the spiritual life. The very first settlers who arrived in 1968 in Pondicherry, South India, were adventurers who believed in a new world order: in the fact that Auroville was a necessity to evolve a new species, wherein a rich collective life was a prerequisite for the individual to progress towards that end.

This monograph series on Auroville architects—*The Pioneers*—emerged from a deep sense of gratitude. Gratitude towards Auroville, that it exists even after 50 years, through all its struggles and limitations, and continues to be an ideal, a concept, a city in the making, nurturing the lives of those who converge here from all over the world. Gratitude also towards those pioneers who came to a barren red plateau and had the conviction to follow a dream, who gave their youth to make it what it is today: a green haven with opportunities for all.

Auroville, 1968

The lack of pre-defined laws and societal norms has allowed a multitude of expressions to manifest in the course of Auroville's development, as natural extensions of the quest for the new, both within and without. The idealism with which Auroville was launched in 1968 and the numerous multifaceted experiments undertaken since the early years in all aspects of architectural expression—from innovative spatial designs using appropriate building materials and technologies to questioning the user's lifestyle; from environment-friendly building infrastructure and cost-effective solutions in a tropical hot-humid climate to research on the relationship between the human organism and the built-form—continues to attract visitors from everywhere.

I was fortunate in conceptualizing and giving form to this series of monographs in 2005, at a time when, about 40 years since its inception, Auroville was ready to look back and introspect critically at where it had reached from those first years of struggle and heady idealism. Fortunate also because it gave me the opportunity to reflect upon and analyse the works of the four pioneering architects of Auroville—Roger Anger (1923–2008), Piero (born 1935) and Gloria Cicionesi (born 1933), and Poppo Pingel (born 1942)—and gain a deeper insight into their approach to work. They have been deeply reticent until now despite numerous attempts at documenting in words their contribution to Auroville. This series began at a time when we were still able to record Roger Anger in his own words, for the first time, before his passing on 15 January 2008.

These pioneering architects come from diverse backgrounds in Europe: France, Italy and Germany respectively. While they have chosen different ways to express themselves, their commitment and dedication to Auroville for a major part of their lives and careers is a common thread. The works of these individual architects, who have created a sufficient body of projects in Auroville, demand serious documentation, analysis of the highlights and failures, and assessment of areas of replicability and relevance; not only for Auroville's own further development but also for the rest of India and the world.

While researching for these monographs through many hours of interviews and archiving, I was often deeply moved and struck by their humility, their simplicity and their straightforward approach to life and their work. For them, working in and for Auroville during these 50 years has been a product of their life's inner aspirations.

> "It is through work that we can detect and progressively get rid of the feelings and movements that are contrary to the yogic ideal: those of the ego."
>
> —Sri Aurobindo

Over many years of living and building in Auroville, I have come to appreciate the foundation that these pioneers have laid for us. They instilled certain values in the Auroville work culture and set standards from which all who come later can profit. Those early years were tough for young aspiring architects. There were no qualified structural engineers, contractors or supervisors, and skilled masons, carpenters, painters or bar-benders were almost non-existent. Building materials available in Pondicherry, 10 km away, were rudimentary and the next big possibility was Chennai, 160 km away. Despite these difficulties and limitations, the buildings that came up in those early years still manage to inspire many: be it Roger's buildings with their curvilinear earth-hugging innovative shapes, the "Aspiration"[1] huts of Piero and Gloria using local know-how in a modern way or Poppo's low-cost "Fraternity"[2] workshops inspired by Japanese simplicity and detailing.

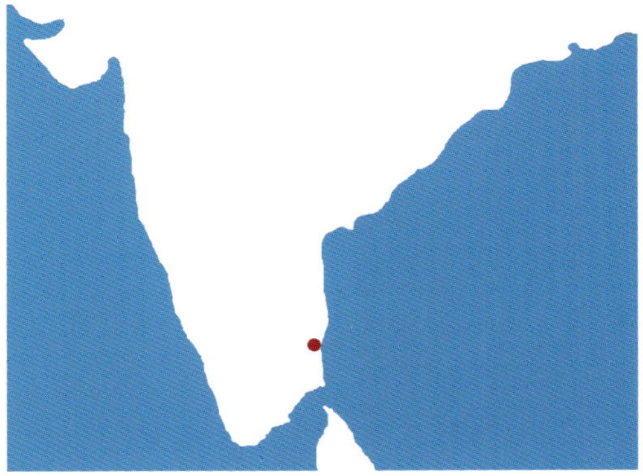

Auroville: 10 km north of Pondicherry and 160 km south of Chennai on the Bay of Bengal

Climatic zone: Tropical hot-humid
Latitude: 11°55' N, Longitude: 70°52'E
Altitude: 50 m above mean sea level
Average annual rainfall: 1,200mm
Average relative humidity: 70–80%
Annual mean minimum temperature: 22°C,
Annual mean maximum temperature: 43°C
Annual mean temperature: 27°C
Annual global solar radiation: 439 cal/sq. cm

Auroville, 2011

Today in Auroville we often take for granted the workmanship of different roofing and flooring possibilities; the quality of rammed earth, exposed brickwork or precast concrete; the ability of the local untrained but enterprising supervisors and contractors to read and understand drawings, as well as their willingness to experiment, to take on new challenges and learn from their mistakes. Masons and carpenters are proud of the work they do in Auroville. A building construction crew with "Auroville experience" commands respect and welcome in megapolises like Bangalore, Chennai or Hyderabad. Changes of this kind in a society do not come in a day and require the persistent effort of many years.

The spirit these pioneers had in those years, of not accepting "no" for an answer and persevering against all odds to achieve a perfection that is a critical part of the "Integral Yoga" of The Mother and Sri Aurobindo[3] has made it possible for us to enjoy today the benefits of the seeds they sowed so many years ago.

Every year several hundred architects visit Auroville searching for inspiration. They look for professional material on Auroville architecture. Yet, little comprehensive material exists on the topic, especially written by architects, particularly Auroville architects.

These monographs are an attempt in this direction. They start by reviewing the works of Auroville's pioneering architects who have contributed to the spirit of innovation, experimentation and perfection, something that has become synonymous with Auroville's architecture scene today. The monographs also archive some of their early works that are fast deteriorating and get their views on record. It is hoped that this series will continue, perhaps with other authors writing about other Auroville architects, and will contribute to an authentic documentation of the significance and influence of Auroville's architectural projects by gathering the achievements made possible in this unique laboratory situation for architectural education.

Fortunately, in the last few years, several new publications have come out on different themes of Auroville's built forms. The first monograph in this series, published in 2012, focused on Poppo Pingel. In the current monograph, we have the added advantage of advanced technology by means of embedded augmented reality videos of Piero and Gloria talking on the Matrimandir and life in Auroville.

Some of my earliest memories of Piero are of approaching him for drawings as a student writing my diploma thesis on the Matrimandir in 1990.[4] He was one of the few who knew at that time about the relationship of proportions between the Great Pyramid and the Matrimandir. He hardly spoke about his difficulties in realizing the Matrimandir with such perfection in the rudimentary conditions of Auroville or of other achievements. Luckily in Auroville, acts count more than words, and the respect that Piero and Gloria garner in the community speak volumes about their humility and dedication to the realization of the Matrimandir and other projects featured in this book. It has been gratifying to see that since the research for this monograph started almost 10 years ago, there has been more interest within Auroville and most importantly a greater articulation from the usually reticent Piero and Gloria in putting on record their journey in Auroville.

Mona Doctor-Pingel,
November 2017

The Context: Auroville—Unfolding of a Vision

The Charter of Auroville

1. Auroville belongs to nobody in particular. Auroville belongs to humanity as a whole. But to live in Auroville one must be a willing servitor of the Divine Consciousness.
2. Auroville will be the place of an unending education, of constant progress, and a youth that never ages.
3. Auroville wants to be the bridge between the past and the future. Taking advantage of all the discoveries from without and from within, Auroville will boldly spring towards future realizations.
4. Auroville will be a site of material and spiritual researches for a living embodiment of an actual Human Unity.

The Mother
28 February 1968

This Charter was given to Auroville as one of its main guidelines by its founder, French-born Mira Alfassa, known as The Mother. She, along with India's great philosopher and yogi Sri Aurobindo, initiated the "Integral Yoga". She joined Sri Aurobindo in 1914 and in 1926 took charge of the fledgling community growing around him, that eventually came to be known as the Sri Aurobindo Ashram, Pondicherry, South India. Sometime around June 1965, The Mother expressed her intention to build Auroville, to actualize the vision and philosophy of Sri Aurobindo.

"Auroville wants to be a Universal town where men and women of all countries are able to live in peace and progressive harmony, above all creeds, all politics and all nationalities. The purpose of Auroville is to realize human unity."

—The Mother
(8 September 1965)

The foundation stone of Auroville was laid on 28 February 1968, in the presence of some 5,000 delegates. Youth from 23 states of India and 124 countries of the world placed a handful of soil from their state/country into a marble-clad urn shaped like a lotus bud "to mingle in it without manmade divisions"[5] in a symbolic gesture. It was during this ceremony that Auroville's Charter was read in different languages: foreign and Indian. There was great expectation of building "The City of Dawn", "The City of the Future". The ground reality was a barren plateau of red laterite earth with a few palm trees, peanut fields, deep canyons caused by erosion over the years, hardly any skilled construction labour, sleepy little villages, where bullock carts, sheep and goats lived amiably, braving dust storms, the blazing scorching sun in the summer and monsoons where the sea became red from the water runoffs.

The City Masterplan

Roger Anger (1923–2008), the French architect, was invited to design this city sometime in 1965. Having been trained in the final post-war era of the original École des Beaux-Arts system, an understanding of architecture as a plastic art had been instilled in him. It was this penchant for formalist composition that would come to define the iconic vision for Auroville.[6]

The extraordinary Galaxy masterplan of Auroville that evolved from a sketch made by The Mother in 1965 has been an inspiration for many. It came at the right time: the youthful idealism of the 1960s was strong and change was in the air: the hippie movement, the students' revolution and the heroic period of the Modern Movement was coming to an end. Young people were searching for new forms to embody a new consciousness.

However, the land designated for the city and the surrounding green belt needed to be purchased. The vast funding required, both for land and construction of the City, did not materialize immediately. As the first Aurovilians began to trickle in and settle down on the land, they learned about the rhythms and culture of the people around them in the villages, who were impoverished and mostly uneducated. Millions of saplings were planted simply as a measure of self-survival from the dust storms and the heat of the vast barren plateau. Slowly, the Galaxy plan—with its huge multistoreyed buildings, monorails and moving sidewalks—appeared more like a distant dream that would take its own time and course in manifesting. Other problems and awakenings at a global level led to further awareness; the oil crisis of the early seventies and the accelerating

Foundation ceremony of Auroville, 28 February 1968

Enhanced with **BooksPlus**

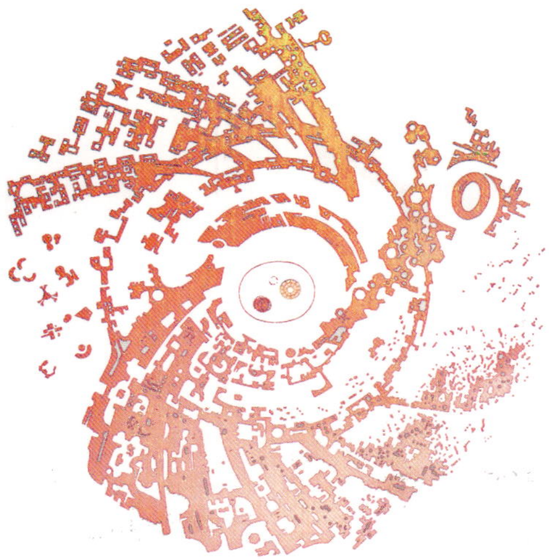

Galaxy plan of Auroville, 1967. Architect Roger Anger and his team in Paris developed several proposals during 1966–68 and presented them to The Mother for approval. They reflected the zeitgeist of the time. Among them were a conventional grid-type plan, the nebula model, the macro-structure model and several forerunners of the Galaxy plan itself. The final circular Galaxy plan is based on a spiralling galaxy divided into four zones with lines of force (low to high rise buildings in a curve), accentuating the galactic movement, and the Matrimandir at the centre. Outside of this Galaxy is a greenbelt also in a circle, almost three times larger in area than the galaxy itself. Within this total plan of 25 sq. km are five existing villages whose total population today is approximately 10,000, while the population of Auroville is 3,000.

environmental movement brought new insights into such idealistic city-planning. Thus, inevitably Auroville began to grow slowly, organically, in a piecemeal manner.

Small-scale, labour-intensive construction along with cultivation, reforestation and various specialized cottage industries seemed more appropriate and sustainable. Moreover, The Mother passed away in November 1973, and that became another milestone for Auroville.

Roger Anger, faced with the responsibility of manifesting the City as envisaged, became increasingly frustrated with the situation. To avoid getting drawn into the power struggle that was then enveloping the township and its residents,[7] he resigned from the main organizing committee in 1975 and ultimately left for France in 1976, returning eventually in 1987 to play an active role once again.[8] In the interim, many difficulties arose, sometimes questioning the very existence of Auroville. Nevertheless it has managed to survive in its spirit and grow on a material level. Auroville, even today, remains an arena of experiment and transformation at all levels of life and humanity, and this is probably the real challenge for its architecture and planning.

Over the years, Auroville has attracted, and continues to attract, people from all over the world. Some leave in the face of difficulties of pioneering something new, others because of the seemingly chaotic system of governance and decision-making with no hierarchical structure. Too much idealism can wear off, as can day-to-day practical difficulties of different cultures living together, where nothing belongs to anybody in particular but to the collective as a whole. Some stay on, never giving up, believing this to be their *karmabhoomi*,[9] believing in the impossible, giving it all they have and in the process moulding themselves, defeating inherent inertia, jumping over their own shadows, trying, experimenting with renewed vigour, sometimes with wisdom, other times with naivety. And so "The City" builds itself slowly but surely.

The envisaged population for the city was 50,000 in 1968. Today, after 50 years, Auroville has a population of approximately 2,300 adults and 700 children from 52 different nations. The villages in and around Auroville have also grown in size and approximately 6,000 villagers are employed in Auroville activities. The relationship with the local people and those who come from elsewhere to make Auroville their home continues to be a complex theme. However, there seems to be more that unites than divides those that reside on and around the Auroville plateau. There is a strong bond born of shared memory, endeavour and a very particular spirit of place.

Not surprisingly, every architect, town planner—every Aurovilian, in fact—begins at some point to ask themselves: "How does one merge the Galaxy concept with the ground realities without losing its essence? What should the process of its building be? Are we going in the right direction? What is our role in the region, India and the world? What is in fact the raison d'être of Auroville? Is this why I came here?" And there are as many answers as there are Aurovilians, and each one has a place in the total puzzle that is Auroville.

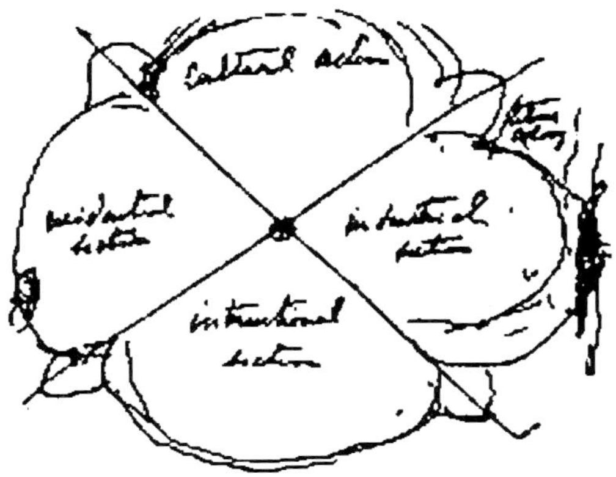

Finally, it is not only the "finished product" but also the "process" followed, both within and without, that is most important in Auroville. It is about living in the present and yet aiming towards a future that seems impossible. Ideally then, the process of building becomes a means of learning and experience wherein all aspects of man's nature—physical, vital, mental as well as the spiritual—are developed and perfected.

When one lives longer in Auroville, experiencing the ups and downs, with idealism and illusions being confronted, checked and reformulated through life experiences, many existential questions arise. One of them is: How has such an experiment been allowed, nurtured and actively supported by the Indian government on Indian soil? One begins then to understand that Auroville *will BE* what it is meant to be in spite of, or because of, all our collective efforts. To live in Auroville is an act of faith.

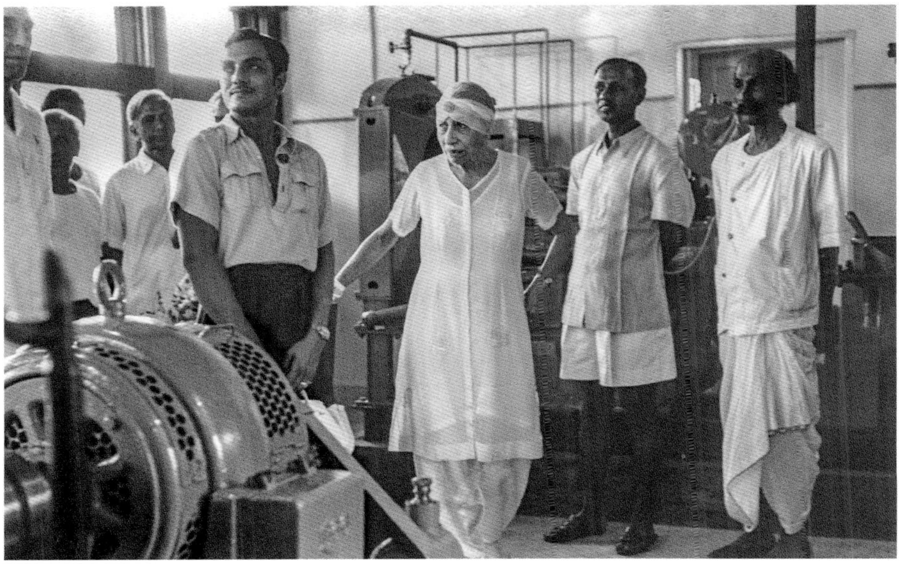

ABOVE
Sketch given by The Mother in 1965, explaining the four zones of Auroville: residential, cultural, industrial and international

BELOW
Mira Alfassa (The Mother, 1878–1973), the founder of Auroville, at the inauguration of a new generator at Sri Aurobindo Ashram Atelier, 12 October 1954

Notes

1. Name of a community within Auroville.
2. Ibid.
3. Integral Yoga stresses a double movement: an ascending aspiration and a descending force. The aim is the divinization of life, a transformation of mind, life and body. Working with spirit and matter, bringing about a perfect balance between the two, is one of the challenges of such a transformation.
4. Mona Doctor, *Form, Structure and Energy - A study of the Matrimandir and The Great Pyramid*, Unpublished diploma thesis, CEPT University, Ahmedabad, 1990.
5. Syril Schochen, "A movement is abroad: An Aurovilian's journey towards the City of Dawn." *Journal of the Integral Yoga of Sri Aurobindo and The Mother* (Collaboration)32, no. 1 (Summer 2007): 9.
6. Vikram Bhatt and Peter Scriver, *Contemporary Indian Architecture: After the Masters* (Ahmedabad: Mapin, 1990).
7. Auroville underwent a protracted period of difficulties with the original nurturing body, the Sri Aurobindo Society in Pondicherry. This culminated in intervention by the Government of India in 1980 and the passing of a special Auroville Foundation Act in 1988 by the Indian Parliament.
8. Extracts from "The Auroville Experience," *Auroville Today*, 2006 and *Auroville Architecture – towards new forms for a new consciousness* (Auroville: Prisma, 2003).
9. Sanskrit word meaning "field of action".

Introduction

Silent Sentinels

Piero and Gloria share a profound sense of life, beauty and simplicity that lends a quietness to their works. Both hail from the magical town of Florence in Italy, and yet, experienced very different formative years. For both, architecture is not only a search for beauty but also has a deeper social aspiration, given the influence of the Leftist cultural milieu in early post-war Europe on them.

Back in his student days, Piero was often concerned with ideas of mediation between rationalism and expressionism, between intellect and artistic intuition. He would discuss these at length with his professor and mentor, Giovanni Klaus Koenig[1] who later wrote an article on the role of the architect's intuition in the process of design, with reference to one of Piero's university projects.[2] Traces of this process of designing can be seen in many of the buildings by Piero and Gloria in Auroville, where a balance between order and freedom has led to various intuitive expressions.

Explaining their method of working, they say: "*The first phase is to make ourselves aware of the functions requested by the project, of their interrelation, their size, the budget, the location, orientation, access... Then we close all this data in a special drawer of the mind (but which is easy to reopen), before they can become an aim in themselves. In this phase the space is like a fluid: it can assume endless shapes. At the same time, we think of the structure, the entrance, the manner of protecting the openings and external walls. One begins to make sketches by hand and a first idea of volumes is generated. In this phase may emerge subconscious memories of details of projects or styles known to us.*"

They especially attribute Luis Barragan[3]—who claims that "...any work of architecture that does

ABOVE
Luis Barragan's Fuente de los Amantes, Mexico

BELOW
View towards the living room of Auroson's Home from outside, with sliding doors folded.

not produce serenity is a mistake"—and Ricardo Legorreta[4] as inspirations in their work because of the similar climate in which they built. "*We like the play of geometry, especially of the volumes in their works.*" Extended gateways, punctures in walls, and other geometric gestures that characterize the works of these renowned architects subtly find their way into the designs of works by Piero and Gloria in Auroville. One can also find influences of Louis Kahn[5] Richard Meier[6] and Erik Kråkström[7] particularly in the manner of dealing with the play of light and shadow, stark volumes and junctions between materials. Deep experiences of living in Finland linger in the background and are expressed through influences from great Finnish masters such as Alvar Aalto[8] and Reima Pietilä[9] as seen in the later explorations of various school buildings.

In 1968, when Piero and Gloria arrived in Auroville directly from Italy with strong impressions from their time in Finland, they were plunged into designing buildings on the barren red plateau with all the problems that a tropical climate brings with it. Additionally Roger Anger, with his Beaux Arts tradition of sculptural forms, who had been appointed as the chief architect of Auroville in 1965, proved a strong influence. The evolution of their work in Auroville shows a marked distinction between projects in the early years and those in the later years. Each project in those early years, when Roger was still available to

LEFT
Piero with the modular model for Service Farm Housing, 1970 (unbuilt project)

RIGHT
Gloria in the studio, working on models of modules for Cluster of Three Houses, 1972

Aspiration community kitchen, 1974

Auroville, had to be shown as a "*maquette*"[10] to him. Piero and Gloria synthesized their fine sense of detail and simple, clean lines with a search for aesthetically dynamic forms, which reflects in projects such as the Health Centre (Phase I) at Aspiration, and various early projects in the Certitude community.

They had followed debates of authors and town planners in the vibrant Italian Leftist cultural milieu of their time and had been taught by professors such as Leonardo Ricci who declared already in 1960: "I think we must give up that which is personal and subjective in favour of that which is collective and objective." Piero and Gloria's works also seem to be about translating such a philosophy of community living into built form. Some significant public projects in Auroville designed by them demonstrates this, including the Aspiration community kitchen various schools and institutional buildings, such as Unity Pavilion. Often one finds that a modular approach using a square or hexagon base as in Aspiration huts or the square-with-rounded-edge as in Andy and Shyamsunder's house allows them to create a play of volumes, light and shadow. The boundary between residential and community life are often blurred, such as in Auroson's Home, where the living room is designed as an extension of the community, with doors sliding open to welcome community meetings in the early years.

The spaces created by Piero and Gloria speak of a spatial quality that is modern, simple and almost timeless in their essence. The duo's belief in simplicity and essentiality correspond with a yogic attitude towards life, which necessitates an elimination of the superfluous. Size, scale and proportions are central principles in architecture, synthesizing mathematics and art. These seem to form the very basis of their design process, evident across their buildings in Auroville. Right from the juxtapositions of masses to the proportions of window grills and door handles... all of these are rigorously and clearly explored through physical models, sketches and 3-D drawings on computer, before the final composition comes together as a harmonious whole. Alluding to the works of Richard Meier, whose works have a rigorous language yet do not exclude the use of free forms and fluid spaces, Piero says, "*For us, proportions and poetry are necessary qualities for a construction to be considered 'architecture'. When one first sees a building, there is a rapidity with which one perceives it. It is firstly an emotional contact and the mind is not present.*"

Linearity, floating roofs and extended free beams are accentuated in their later projects. One also sees them embracing new materials that were not available in the early years in Auroville. In their previous works, they were free from concerns about mosquitoes, termites, insects, rodents and thieves. In their later projects, amidst an ever-increasing population, one sees a growing acknowledgement of the needs of the physically aging residents and concerns about the insect world and security. On a couple of projects, such as Rika's and Ilse's house, where Gloria was more involved, one can see such concerns coming prominently to the fore while also bringing a nuanced sensitivity towards details, reflecting her graceful and warm character.

Piero's role in Auroville's history remains unique. He was given the task to execute and build the Matrimandir—Auroville's physical and spiritual centre—when he was just 36. He continued this work for 20 years persistently with patience and faith, until the Inner Chamber was completed to the last detail in 1992. His mathematical genius combined with his sense of perfection and material detailing came to the fore, was sharpened and often put to test in the democratic, collective milieu of Auroville. It was not for nothing that Piero was one of the best students during his years at the architecture school in Florence, where he passed the Structural Science exams with "maximum cum laude".

The story of the Matrimandir can be recalled and retold in many ways and from different perspectives. This book attempts to follow Piero's journey in the manifestation of the Matrimandir. This work called forth from Piero a hidden potential and made him into a master builder/architect–engineer in the Vitruvian sense: someone who can combine science and art, is skilful with the pencil, is educated in geometry, is concerned with craftsmanship and philosophy, and is acquainted with astronomy and the inherent laws of movement of the cosmos. Someone who is able to command a team of voluntary workers from all walks of life to create a superbly finished work harmoniously.

Piero and Gloria live a rich yet simple life and, like their buildings, do not call for attention but simply

FORMATIVE YEARS

Piero and Gloria Cicionesi

Piero Cicionesi

Born in 1935, just before the troubled war years in Italy, Piero recalls his childhood and early family life with a sense of fondness, more appropriately described as a sense of "Gemütlichkeit!"[1]

His early education was in a German school, under the influence of his German mother. Towards the end of the Second World War, the school was closed down and the teachers had to flee. Piero and his brother were shifted to an Italian school in Florence. He reminisces, *"When I was a boy I showed a special talent in design, in drawings, in painting, in colour, and when I discovered this myself I was 14 or 15 years old. I still have a vivid memory of my first drawings and, by chance, they were linked with architecture. They were of houses, old houses... a bit picturesque probably. I tried oil colours and then watercolour paintings..."*

In those post-war formative years, the paintings of Filippo de Pisis[2] left a deep impression on Piero's young mind. He recalls, *"The paintings of Pisis impressed me very much. I had seen a big exhibition in Florence on him. I was very impressed because he had these very rapid strokes of the brush. In three-four strokes it was already defined. I tried out painting in that manner."*

Another early attribute was Piero's proficiency in mathematics, one that grounded the artist in him with a rational, logical understanding of structure. Many years later, it was this synthesis of art and math that emerged strongly when Piero began work on the complex structural drawings of the Matrimandir in Auroville.[3]

Piero recalls an exhibition organized by a renowned Italian critic in 1951 on the "Life Work of Frank Lloyd Wright" that left a deep impact on his mind.

PAGE 28
Sand-mining flatboat on River Po, Turin, ink drawing on paper.

ABOVE
City of Florence

LEFT
Watercolour painting, Piero, 1952

RIGHT
Oil painting, Filippo de Pisis, 1896–1956

ABOVE
Falling Water, Frank Lloyd Wright

BELOW
'Garden of Sculptures', designed by Carlo Scarpa at the Venice Biennale, 1952

The exhibition had models, original sketches and drawings displayed in a famous gallery of Florence. In Piero's words, *"I saw his drawings and was touched by the experience of seeing the harmony, which was so much in contrast to the chaos of colour and form that I was to see later in the art at the Venice Biennale. The impressive architecture of Wright coming out of these vivid, mostly pencil, drawings was a language that I was able to read and intuitively understand. I felt I would like to do that too. I learned to describe the experience much later, through the words of critic Paul Goldberger, who said about one of Wright's most celebrated creations, Falling Water: 'Like any kind of great art, it ultimately takes you somewhere that words cannot take you.' And it was in 1952, when I was 17, that I decided to go to Venice for the Biennale."*

The Venice Art Biennale had an international exhibition of modern paintings. The young, idealistic Piero took a train and reached Venice with a sketchbook in hand. The Biennale left him shocked by the sheer range and quantity of work. *"It was like a maze. The jungle of abstract, formal, informal, and all kinds of artwork was an overwhelming experience and I felt like an outsider with my modest sketching and painting,"* says Piero. However, by chance, the Biennale also introduced him to the original and imaginative works of Italian architect Carlo Scarpa.

Describing the experience, Piero recounts, *"Scarpa had designed a Pavilion and restored an old building for the exhibition with a fantastic intuition. You have a very well-defined way through the maze of paintings and at its end, you find suddenly a round opening. You reach the opening and what do you see there? The blue water of the canal, gently cooling off your agitated mind! That sort of a surprise element! You see an amazing and elegant free form—a roof resting only on three points and a small courtyard—and you discover something new, a sort of mysterious emotion coming from it. In 1952, I was not able to read and understand properly these forms and details. I learned much later that I was in the so-called 'Garden of Sculptures' that Scarpa had just completed. A sculpture in itself! I was not an architect then, but I was completely taken by these new emotions."*

Sometime around 1932, the city of Florence decided to build a new railway station.[4] It was a competition project, recalls Piero. In the pre-war years, the various

LEFT
Venezuelan pavilion for the Venice Biennale, 1954–56, designed by Carlo Scarpa

RIGHT
Sketches by Piero for a project in his university days, published by Professor Giovanni Klaus Koenig in support of his essay on the role of the architect's intuition in the process of design (see p. 21). The numbers indicate stages in the design process.

Streets of Helsinki, wax pastels on paper by Piero, 1962

FACING PAGE

LEFT

Cathedral in Florence, 1956, ink and watercolour on paper by Piero

RIGHT

Cathedral in Siena, 1957, ink and watercolour on paper by Piero

ABOVE, FACING PAGE AND FOLLOWING PAGE
Piero's ball-point pen sketches on handmade paper, 1974

designs by different architects reflected the confusions of a Neo-Classical or an imitative Gothic style. The building designs were compromised by stylistic gestures rather than content, purity of structure and form that the Modern Movement espoused. Architect Giovanni Michelucci[5] (1891–1990) and his young associates had submitted a stark modernist design. Unable to decide between old and new styles, the jury had requested Mussolini himself to choose the winning design. Michelucci's design was selected. *"The Santa Maria Novella Railway Station marked the arrival of Modern Architecture in Florence,"* recalls Piero, who had the opportunity of meeting the legendary architect several years later. Michelucci and Carlo Scarpa worked on several museum renovations in Florence after the war. The rich craftsmanship and detailing of such buildings around them has had a great influence on Piero and Gloria.

"I think it was in those years, at the age of four or five, and in the same station, that a new word— 'modern'— must have been added to my limited vocabulary from conversations of grownups around me. For me, it was more than learning a word. It came to represent an enjoyable and positive experience each time we passed the station. So 'modern', for a long time, remained connected with these moments and this experience." In a very subconscious and intuitive way, these experiences could have influenced Piero's decision to become an architect.

Much of Piero's early experiences in a stark post-war Europe of the 20th century strengthened his belief in a simple and logical architecture, synthesizing the rational with the artistic. *"It could be the influences of a German mother and an Italian father,"* Piero light-heartedly reminisces.

His father, a musician in the early part of the 20th century, always reminded his twin sons what he told his students of music: to pursue excellence and not succumb to laziness. "There is no space for in-between, there is no space for mediocrity," his father would say. These words have remained with Piero, ingrained in his thoughts and guiding his practice.

Gloria Buffi

Born in 1933, Sundays in Gloria's childhood were spent visiting museums and churches of Florence with her parents, elder sister and younger brother Giampiero, who too became a well-known architect. She particularly remembers visiting the Gothic Church of Santa Croce: *"I remember this enormous space with its Giotto School frescos, the light streaming in from the top and the grand courtyard of the old monastery. I was enchanted. Even today I enjoy very much the rays of sun piercing through the leaves in nature. I carry this within myself."*

Once, while visiting an Etruscan museum at the age of 10 or 12, she saw the reconstruction of a dome used for burials. She remembers her interest in the unusual way it was built: concentric rings of flat stones decreasing in diameter to form a dome. How could it stand like that? To see for herself, she came home and built a small dome in the garden with pebbles, and managed to make it stand! Her mother—a teacher and believer in women's emancipation—was encouraging and appreciative of Gloria's budding curiosity in buildings.

The awareness of growing up in a place as historical and beautiful as Florence has remained a foundation for her. Summer holidays were spent at the family's little "goat barn" on the island of Elba in the idyllic setting of rural Tuscany. Gloria would often express herself through poems inspired by the beauty of nature.

During the war period, Gloria stayed in Siena with her family for three months. On her experience, she comments: *"I was about 10, and loved the architecture of the Middle Ages and its natural fluid development inside the walled town."*

Gloria was enamoured by the works of Scarpa, Mies van der Rohe, Frank Lloyd Wright and Alvar Aalto in her college days. Later, when she discovered the work of Louis Kahn, she found it absolutely touching that despite being inspired by ancient architecture,

LEFT
Gloria Buffi, 1966
Enhanced with BooksPlus

RIGHT
A detail of the Indian Institute of Management, Ahmedabad, building, designed by Louis Kahn, 1961.

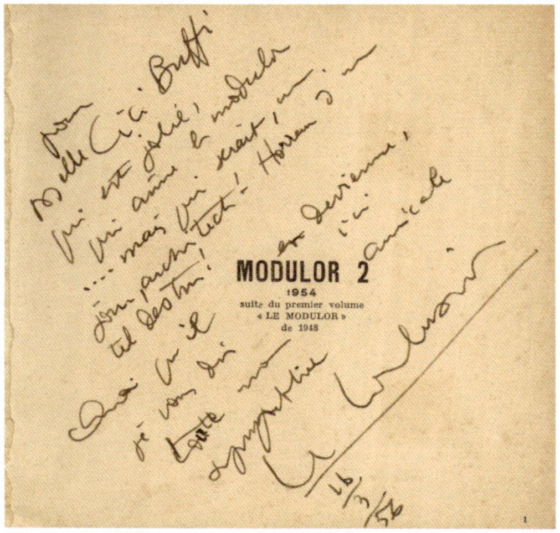

Le Corbusier's autographed note to Gloria, 1956

he managed to create something totally new with a sense of the sacred, the play of light and shadow, the stillness and depth of his spaces. Speaking about what inspires her, Gloria says, *"For me, it's the poetry of architecture that is fascinating. Louis Kahn describes it as something between silence and light. I find this poetic definition captures the essence of architecture."*[15] Scarpa's work also fascinates her for its superb detailing, where different materials come together in perfect harmony.

In 1956, Gloria was in Paris while studying architecture and Francois Le Lionnais—a mathematician and scientist, friend of Gloria's family, who helped Corbusier with the formulation of the Modulor—brought her for a short visit to the office of Le Corbusier. She, as a woman, was not allowed into the studio space, since Corbusier found women in his office to be a bit of a "distraction". However, he joked with Gloria about whether she had worked with Brunelleschi, since she came from Florence and graciously signed her a personal copy of the Modulor :

To Mademoiselle Cici Buffi,
Who is nice, and who loves the Modulor, who one day will be an Architect. Horror of such a destiny...!
Does not matter what she will become. I want to tell her, all my friendly sympathy."

—Le Corbusier
16 March 1956

Mentors

Both Piero and Gloria went to the same high school (though in different classes) and eventually studied Architecture at the University of Florence, during 1954–61, which was known for its excellent curriculum and dedicated teachers. Giovanni Michelucci (1891–1990) was one of its prime directional forces in the formative years till he resigned in 1948 with a letter titled "The Happiness of an Architect".[7] The university's tough curriculum also included two years of Structural Science, based on theory of elasticity and design, and calculation of beams and frames. The tests for the theory of mechanical forces, which were considered most difficult, were those in which Piero excelled, each time securing maximum marks.

Piero's skills in drawing were soon recognized and encouraged at the university. He had done a few drawings for architectural firms in Florence during his final years. Hearing about his skills, Michelucci called Piero when he was in his fourth year and commissioned him to do a perspective of a tower block in Livorno, a town near Florence. It was considered a privilege and an honour. Later, Piero graduated as the best student in his academic year. Impressed with Piero's capacity, Michelucci eventually invited him to come again when he was designing one of his most challenging

works: Chiesa dell' Autostrada. However, Piero was at that time in Finland and wrote him a postcard that he could unfortunately not come.

Several of Michelucci's former students taught at the Architecture Academy, such as Leonardo Savioli (1917–81), Edorado Detti (1913–84), Domenico Cardini (1913–95), Giuseppe Gori (1906–69), Italo Gamberini (1907–90), Giovanni K. Koenig (1924–89). They taught town planning, history of architecture and architecture of composition respectively.

However, Piero's and Gloria's favourite teacher was Leonardo Ricci (1918–94), who had also been a student of Michelucci. Known for his flamboyant personality that attracted students to him, Leonardo Ricci was "an architect, an artist, a teacher, but above all a visionary, profoundly concerned with the state of the twentieth-century man in, what he considered to be, a time of transition between an old civilisation and a new civilisation struggling to be born. He lived in Florence, Italy, but he had also lived in Paris and in the United States, where he was a visiting lecturer on architecture at the MIT."[8] Gloria reminisces, *"During our university years we were introduced to a certain conception of space by Professor Ricci: a fascinating personality full of passion for architecture and humanity."* Remembering Ricci's architecture, Piero recalls, *"I was struck by his bold use of natural stone walls, concrete beams or slabs and simple glass enclosures."*

ABOVE LEFT
Piero's sketch of Fontana di Trevi, ink and watercolour, 1958

ABOVE RIGHT
Tower block in Livorno, Florence, 1960, a perspective drawing of which Piero did for Michelucci while he was in fourth year of studies

BELOW
Chiesa dell'Autostrada, designed by Michelucci and built in 1963. Michelucci lived to a hundred years and in his later years became increasingly unconventional and innovative.

In 1960, Ricci wrote, "I think that we must get away from the bizarre, the experimental, from the urge to be original at any cost, and search, with due humility, for that which is really essential to the enhancement of our daily existence… I think that we must find an enjoyment of living, that is a reality of living all our own. Only then—outside of myths, ideas, preconceived notions and everything that smacks of a priori—can we create architecture and painting to harmonize with the lives we are leading, no longer as symbols but as meaningful, existential acts."[9]

ABOVE AND FACING PAGE Casa-studio, Monterinaldi, Florence, by Leonardo Ricci (1952). Echoes of the staircase can be found many years later in Certitude cluster houses.

BELOW Leonardo Ricci

In 1970, Ricci became dean of the Florence Faculty of Architecture. After three years, he was exhausted and left for Venice. An excerpt from an interview with Leonardo Ricci, where he is asked what he thinks of architecture and painting, reveals his constant dialogue about society and the arts: "I think that we have not yet built 'our city', in other words that we have not found a new and completer form of expression. Only a new urbanistic reality can give rise to architecture, painting, and sculpture that we can call truly ours…"

In his old age, Ricci recognized that he had been too optimistic about his dream of a new architecture for a new man. When Piero and Gloria reached Auroville in 1968, this dream of a new man with a new consciousness was, however, rekindled with the words of The Mother (1 August 1954): "New words are needed to express new ideas New forms are necessary to manifest new forces."

CHANCE ENCOUNTER

Piero even today jokes that Gloria is one of the most passionate architects he has ever met. *"She even married an architect… and inspired her younger brother to follow her footsteps!"*

An outcome of Piero being so good in drawing and sketching was that the two had an unusual opportunity to meet. Gloria, who was Piero's senior by a year at the university, needed help for her thesis drawings. Having heard of Piero's skills, she requested if he would

oblige! And that was the beginning of a 60-year relationship that continues to nurture both of them.

However, by the time Piero graduated cum laude, Gloria was travelling and working abroad. On finishing her architecture studies in 1960, as one of only seven women students in the college at the time, she took a well-deserved break at her family's country house in the island of Elba. In 1961, Gloria went to Cologne to work with the German architect Ernst Neufert Jr. She remembers fondly the great Gothic Koelner Dom there with the Rhein flowing next to it. Germany fascinated her with its churches and precision. Next, she worked for a few months with a furniture company in Soest, a small ancient town in Westfalia, designing for them. Again, the St Maria zur Wiese Kirche, a Gothic church in green sandstone, remains with her for the quality of light streaming in.

The same year, Gloria went to Paris where she started working with Georges (Gheorghios) Candilis (1931–95), who had worked with Corbusier as the project architect for the Unité d'habitation in Marseille (1945–52). His office was on a prime location near Pont Neuf, the oldest standing bridge across the Seine. She remembers taking her lunch sitting on the riverfront, visiting her favourite church Sainte-Chapelle (13th century), enjoying this prime example of Rayonnant Gothic style, with its filigreed columns and stained-glass windows flooding the space with a special light. The atmosphere in the office was very international, which she enjoyed. It was here that Piero came looking for Gloria to invite her to Finland, a country which he visited during his university days and which he found to be very special, special enough to travel there again with Gloria.

Scandinavian Lessons

Piero recalls, *"I wanted us to work together and share this experience, especially because of the Alvar Aalto buildings that I liked very much."* The couple set off to Finland in August of 1961 and travelled to Helsinki to visit Alvar Aalto's office. *"An Italian architect—Federico Marconi*[10] *who became later one of the leading architects in the north-east of Italy—working in Alvar Aalto's office suggested that we stay on and work in Helsinki. It was relatively easy to find some work in the offices of the Helsinki architects, who were taking in foreign students and young architects. It was a way of keeping in contact with, what appeared to us then, an international crowd. 'Why not?' we thought, and decided to stay on and work in Finland.*

"Evidently, the main attraction was Alvar Aalto's buildings. But then, we were confronted with other extraordinary architects as well. These architects were choosing intentionally to make very straightforward volumes and simple structures. Finland was like a special Island because Russia is on one side and the sea is on the other three sides.

"Then the Nature, the lakes, the snow, the skiing and the solitude finally convinced Gloria and I to remain at length in Finland. It was a very special time and a rich experience."

ABOVE
Protestant Church, 1961, Piero's graduation project at university

BELOW
Boarding school for difficult children, 1960, Gloria's graduation project at university

Eventually, Piero and Gloria joined the offices of Ola Tomisto and Erik Kråkström respectively. They imbibed the Scandinavian spirit of good design and detailing in these years, which remains evident in their Auroville projects.

In general, the couple's sojourn in Finland was not only about design and architecture, but it was also a social experience. They decided to get married while in Finland. Significant in their Scandinavian experience was an appreciation of a defined balance and quietness, and the simplicity of the homes there that bring a sense of contentment, efficiency and beauty through sensitivity to details.

Piero's disciplined life in the exploration of art and engineering became the foundation for his later journey. To this day, his design aesthetic emerges from function, material and technology, and is subdued even as it is a clear statement, expressing all the elements. For a very long period in his architectural search, Piero preferred a monastic white for their projects, with clear lines that carried forward the simplicity of the Scandinavian experience shared with Gloria.

ABOVE
Säynätsalo Town Hall by Alvar Aalto, Finland, 1949

BELOW
Inside Studio Aalto, Helsinki, 1956

FACING PAGE

LEFT ABOVE
Golconde Dormitories, Pondicherry, in 2008. Designed by Antonin Raymond, Frantisek Sammer and George Nakashima and built between 1935–42, it was one of the first examples of modern architecture in India and is a great example of climate-responsive design.

LEFT CENTRE
Promesse, one of the first communities of row houses in Auroville, where Piero and Gloria stayed for five years, designed by Roger Anger, 1968

LEFT BELOW
Piero and Gloria with daughters Marta and Grazi, Promesse, 1970

RIGHT AND PAGE 51
drawings in ink by Piero, 1962–74

AUROVILLE: A LEAP OF FAITH

During his stay in Finland, Piero had chanced upon a book on Auschwitz by Primo Levi.[13] It gave him a deep shock: *"How could Germany, from a culture of musicians, writers, poets and philosophers, fall into the abyss of a racial perversion like this?"* A wave of deep emotion engulfed Piero at that time. *"Maybe as a reaction, I suddenly started to see faces of people in a different way. It was like entering a different world and I started to draw that. Without knowing anything about the philosophy, I called the sketches 'the Eye of the Buddha', as, for me, it was like discovering the way Buddha saw the people: with compassion, understanding, sharpness.*

"And then, as time passed, this connection with Eastern philosophy suddenly was becoming a reason to come to India: the 'inner force' that was guiding me to come to Auroville. I was confident and did not have any fears or doubts. As far as I remember, at that time in Italy, there were no printed translations of Sri Aurobindo or The Mother's books. Nata, an Italian disciple, was sending us a few notes from the Ashram in Pondicherry: some extracts in a bulletin that he had started to print with a stencil machine, called 'Domani'. We had read a few pages from The Life Divine, but that was enough!"[14]

Piero and Gloria had planned to be in Auroville for its Founding ceremony on 28 February 1968, but the processing of their visas in Rome took much longer than anticipated, and they arrived a week later, in the first week of March.

On their arrival in Pondicherry, Gloria remembers meeting a few ashramites from Sri Aurobindo Ashram, whom she describes, as being *"amazingly sympathetic and kind"*, making them feel *"at home"*. After four days in Pondicherry, they moved to Promesse with their young daughter Marta, where Nata had prepared a place for the family. Promesse was one of the first communities in Auroville, designed by Roger Anger as row housing with courtyards and asbestos roofing. In the spirit of The Mother's teachings, they immediately got involved in the daily life at Auroville, taking up responsibilities of small construction projects.

Piero narrates, *"When we arrived, India was quite different from what it is today. We found a connection on an inner level. It was very personal. It was a spiritual place and offered us the possibility to pursue a disciplined new way of life, of meditation. We saw India as a land of ashrams, and that was very important to us. We experienced these special places in our visits to Ramana Maharishi Ashram, the Theosophical society at Madras and many years later at Santiniketan in West Bengal when we were called to design the Tagore Arts Museum in 1985. But perhaps this connection had indirectly started long before...*

"We resonated with the Auroville Charter and the building of a new city that The Mother wanted for the transformation of consciousness to hasten the advent of a new species. When Gloria and I saw 'Golconde' in Pondicherry, we realized that The Mother wanted Auroville to be a special place, not an ordinary place.

"Towards the end of 1969, we heard about this mysterious building called the Matrimandir."

Little did Piero know that it would become his life's work for the next 20 years.

that the professional works of Piero and Gloria also intrinsically carry these principles of harmony and beauty. Sharing this common background with them, I have to admit that till today, they are my favourite architects here in Auroville.

The Faculty of Architecture in Florence today remains one of the top faculties in Italy, together with that of Venice, which is focused more on Urban Design. Students graduating from these universities have established a good reputation and are equipped with a keen sense for modern architectural principles. I believe that Piero and Gloria are protagonists of the Modernist Movement, shaping their projects primarily through a criterion of functionality rather than just aesthetics, in the manner of Rationalists' works and classical buildings. "Classical" architecture is here understood not as mere mimetic reference to a specific historical period—Renaissance or other—but rather in its timelessness whereby the desire to seek an order, a measure, and a modulation renders the architectural forms clearly perceptible in the light of the sun, as parts of a whole ensemble.

It is not a coincidence that one of the latest works of Piero and Gloria, the Unity Pavilion[3] amply reflects this concept, which is very dear to Michelucci. From him, they have learned to base each design concept on the human being, his scale, his gestures and his necessities. According to Michelucci, architecture wants to be, more than anything, a living organism akin to what we aspire for here in Auroville.

Notes

1. Giovanni Michelucci (1891–1991). Became Dean of the Faculty of Architecture in Florence in 1944.
2. Leonardo Ricci (1918–94). An Italian architect who graduated from the Faculty of Architecture in Florence in 1941. Giovanni Michelucci, his mentor, hired him as an assistant in his studio, where he remained until 1946.
3. See 'Unity Pavilion', p. 175.

Watercolour sketch of
Florence by Piero, 1955

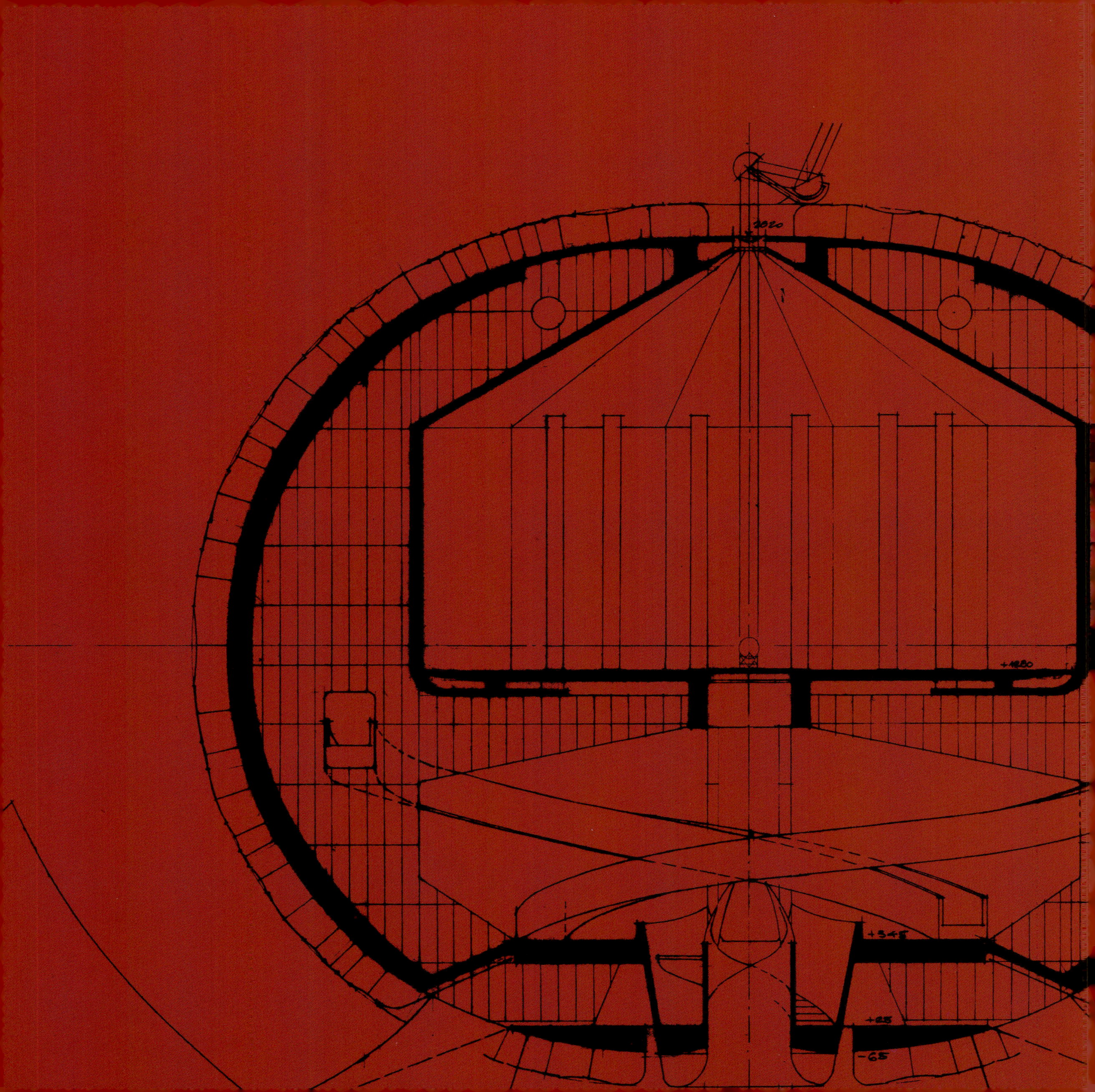

2020
+345
-65

MANIFESTING MATRIMANDIR

The Lone Banyan Tree

There is a point at which all the roads in Auroville, the paths seen and unseen meet, converge and having no place further to travel spatially, turn within. This point is the Matrimandir, the centring of the city.[1]

By early 1967, time had come to define the location of Auroville. After exploring several alternative locations, Roger Anger, the French architect appointed by The Mother to plan and design Auroville City, brought her a map of an area north of Pondicherry, on the way to Madras (now Chennai) to ask her where the centre of Auroville should be. She concentrated and pointed to a particular area on the map.

Driving to the place she had pointed at on the map, Roger found a lone banyan tree there approximately on the highest point of a nearly barren plateau 60 m above sea level, overlooking the Bay of Bengal. The banyan tree is regarded as sacred in India. The Mother was very happy to know of its presence there, and decided to make it Auroville's geographical centre.[2]

Symbolism

At the centre of Auroville, The Mother envisioned a "Park of Unity"[3] containing a "Pavilion of Truth", or "Pavilion of [Divine] Love", or "Pavilion of The Mother".

Galaxy model of Auroville city by Roger Anger, 1967

As the vision manifested itself over various iterations, eventually she named this pavilion "Matrimandir: The Mother's Shrine", in reference to the Universal Mother as the Creator, according to Sri Aurobindo's teaching. It would represent the "soul of Auroville".[4] It is a rarity in today's modern town-planning approaches that a city builds itself around a spiritual symbol, holding this centre in utmost reverence, as a source of all its multifarious aspirations. Therefore, the importance of the Matrimandir to the realization of Auroville's ideals cannot be underestimated.

The Matrimandir, the lone banyan tree and an urn shaped like a lotus bud—standing as the *mundi* of an amphitheatre—together create a powerful ensemble. The Matrimandir represents symbolism of different kinds from those that are mundane to those of highest spiritual significance. Visually, it is perceived as a large and slightly flattened golden sphere suspended over the ground, appearing to rise out of the earth—seeking to burst forth—symbolizing the birth of a new consciousness. Emerging from the "*subconscient*", the subterranean layers break the *tamas*[5] deep in the earth and soar towards the symbolic ray of the sun that shines right from the top to the bottom, signifying the aspiration of man ascending upwards and the corresponding Grace that descends.[6]

Functionally, the purpose of the Matrimandir is to provide a space for concentration, devoid of any religious connotations. The Inner Chamber of the Matrimandir was envisioned by The Mother herself in

Model of Matrimandir by Roger Anger, displayed at the foundation ceremony, 21 February 1971

Enhanced with BooksPlus

Auroville Founding Day Anniversary celebration at Matrimandir. The Matrimandir, the lone Banyan tree and the lotus urn together symbolize the convergence of three world energies, 2005.

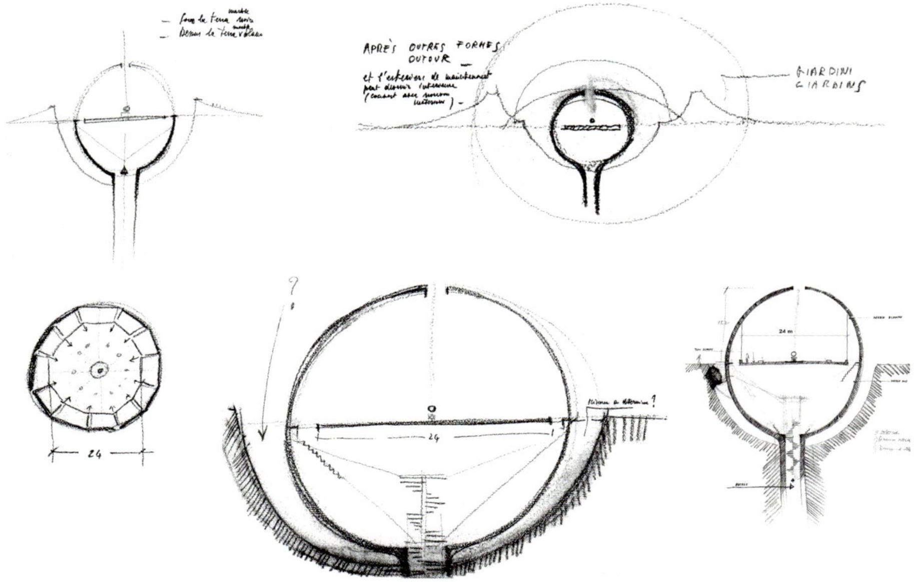

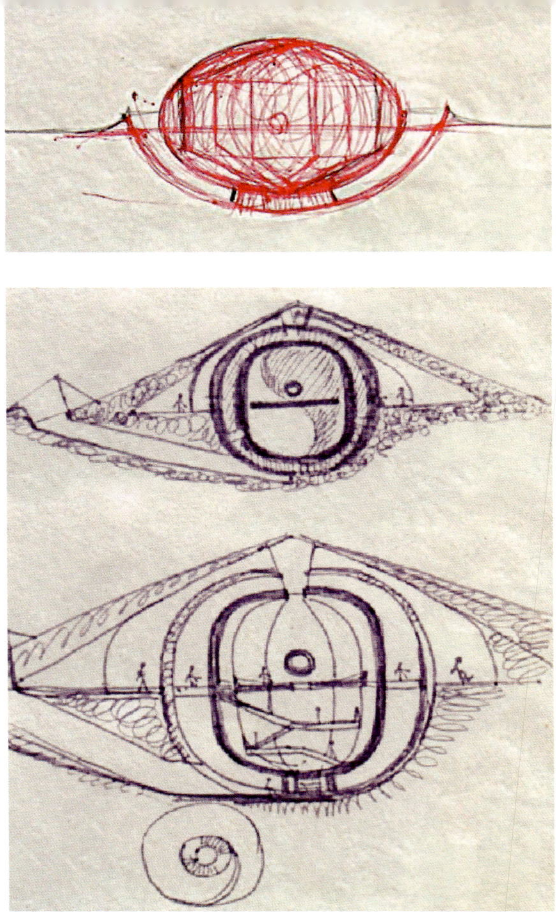

LEFT
Sketches by Paolo Tommasi, based on The Mother's vision, 1969

RIGHT
Roger Anger's sketches for the form of Matrimandir, 1970

great detail and she gave corresponding instructions over many conversations that were recorded and then translated into drawings. She described the Matrimandir as the "living symbol of Auroville's aspiration for the Divine" and as "the central cohesive force of Auroville".

From its foundation, the Matrimandir took 37 long years (21 February 1971–21 February 2008) to complete. It is a labour of love, handcrafted piece by piece and funded by a slow but steady stream of donations. Each aspect of the design was researched in detail and, each time, the best possible solution was taken forward to a perfect manifestation with no thought to any constraints of money, time or labour.

At the end of 1969, Italian architect and The Mother's disciple, Paolo Tommasi, felt that the Matrimandir should be built at the earliest. Her close disciple Satprem conveyed this to her and many conversations followed with him, with Paolo and with Roger Anger, whom she asked to begin working on the design.

Apart from these conversations, some of which were made public four years later[7] one more document was also made available: an accurate measured drawing of the Inner Chamber, as seen by The Mother in repeated visions. The drawing was made by Udar, an aeronautical engineer and long-time ashramite. It was of a 12-sided hall (diameter: 24 m) with 12 columns, at the centre of which was a transparent, translucent object of concentration, illuminated by a vertical ray of sun.

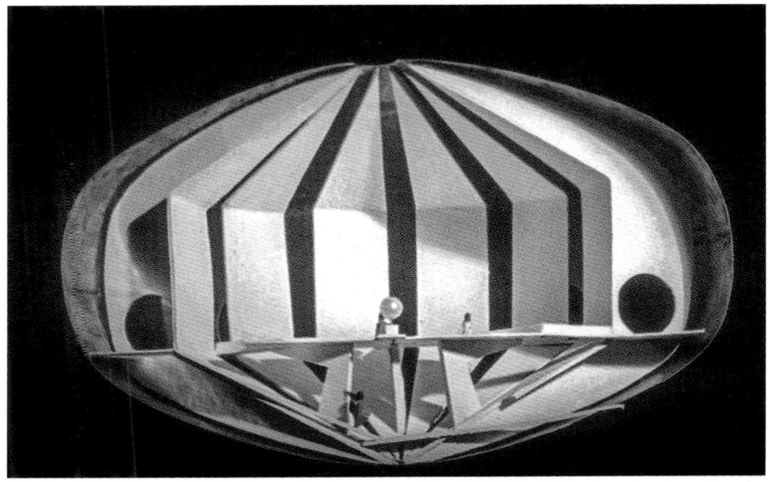

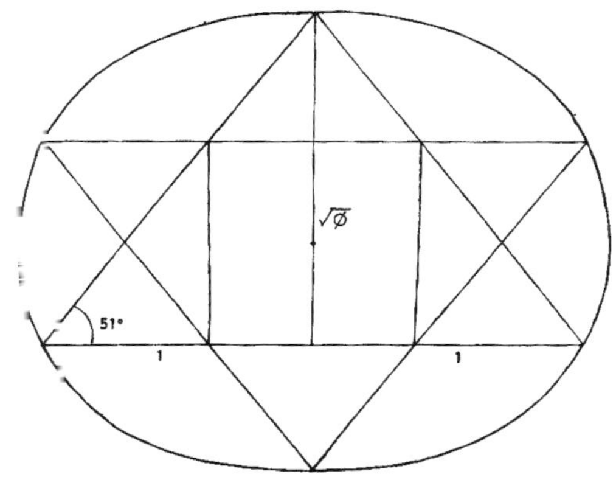

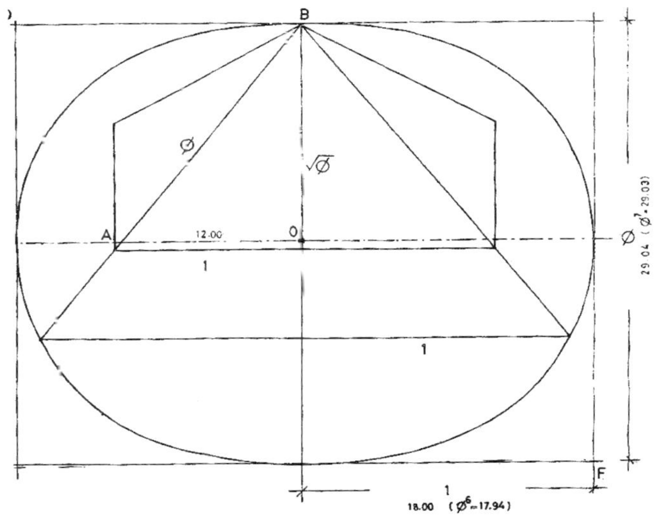

ABOVE LEFT

Early model by Roger Anger—a brass pot representing the Matrimandir, which The Mother selected, 1970

ABOVE RIGHT

Half-model of Inner Chamber of Matrimandir by Roger Anger, presented 24 March, 1970

BELOW: LEFT AND RIGHT

Analysis drawn by Piero between the shape of Shaligram—Sri Aurobindo's symbol, the Matrimandir with Inner Chamber and the Great Pyramid of Giza in Egypt

While The Mother envisioned the space, she wanted Roger and Paolo to work together in defining the form embodying that space and they both made their contributions initially. The result was the shared idea to shape the building in the unique form of a sphere emerging from the earth. Other than that, their visions were different and eventually Roger Anger worked further to conceptualize the project. In March 1970, Roger presented a model of the Inner Chamber along with five different models for the Matrimandir. The Mother selected a slightly flattened golden sphere, to be worked upon further. In 1971, the final approved globe model for the structure was presented to The Mother and to the residents of Auroville. Work could finally start.

Interestingly, the architect chose the shape of a Shaligram[8]—an ancient tantric symbol for the "the unity of creation"—as the final external form (horizontal diameter: 36 m; height: 29 m). Coincidently, unknown to Roger, the proportions of this outer form and the Inner Chamber correspond with the proportions of the Great Pyramid of Giza[9] and Sri Aurobindo's symbol. Matrimandir's exact axis was decided by the position of the rising sun on 4 April, the day Sri Aurobindo arrived in Pondicherry in 1910. Thus, the east–west axis is rotated by 5 degrees anticlockwise.

The Matrimandir Construction

1971–1991

Piero recounts the early days when there was much anticipation and inspiration in Auroville to dedicate oneself to the service of building the Matrimandir: to realize a symbol embodying "the soul" of the city. In the years to follow, the inspired Auroville community volunteered in its construction along with the neighbouring village communities who worked as paid labour. Manifesting the Matrimandir was an act of immense faith, which often appeared daunting and beyond human capacity. There were intense discussions about whether the Aurovilians—a bunch of idealistic, sometimes unruly persons from different countries and all walks of life—had the expertise to build it or if external professional contractors should be assigned the task. An old-time Aurovilian recounts the experience of digging the great crater 10 m into the ground that was to receive the large sphere:

"There was no hubris in this act... Lots of laughter... No one seemed reluctant to go out into the midday sun for something they thought they might not even see completed. The pit was something that needed to be dug; we felt just lucky to be digging it."[10]

Piero recalls the early days when the construction of the Matrimandir had not yet begun but there was talk of a building at the centre:

"The year 1970 began for us—Gloria and I—with the overwhelming experience of reading a copy of some 50-odd typewritten pages dealing with the design of this till-then mysterious building called the Matrimandir, which a friend from the Ashram unexpectedly lent us to read. It was, and still is, an extraordinary document describing in the words of The Mother the details of her vision for the futuristic marvellous building which was to be at the centre of Auroville. For us, it was difficult to perceive all that, given our rudimentary daily life at that time, but we were moved. It was also clear that something big was starting to take shape.

"I came in the picture later, in 1971, when more Aurovilians wanted to collaborate and start to dig the

ground for the future foundations. I remember that, all of a sudden, the project needed urgently one person to oversee the engineering requirements and I was called in by Dr Chamanlal Gupta, a professor and building physicist from the Ashram in Pondicherry. In essence, I was to follow the project of Roger and interact with the structural engineers. Eventually, I was also to mediate between the diametrically opposing demands from the side of Roger and the engineers."

When Piero was eventually entrusted with the responsibility of the detailed working drawings and the construction of the Matrimandir, it appeared to be a daunting task, particularly considering the

ABOVE
Piero with Alain Grandcolas, who was managing the team of diggers at excavation site, 1972

BELOW
Excavation work, 1971

Enhanced with BooksPlus

recalls their role: "*I was working more like a labourer on the site, taking care of all the measurements. To transmit the calculations of the engineers to the workers through the means of drawing... that was done by Piero.*"[12]

The footings were cast in June 1972 and by November of that year all the pillars were concreted up to ground level. Piero narrates those inspired moments of construction shared with volunteering Aurovilians and ashramites: "*We were doing the concreting at night, and people were coming from Pondicherry enthusiastically. Ladies in white saris bringing stones and sand to the mixer machine or making long chains to shift the concrete in the old way, with* chetties[13]*... it appeared magical and anything was possible! It was nice and completely unexpected, because the idea was that we wished the Aurovilians to build the Matrimandir, and then suddenly there were ashramites coming and asking when the next concreting was, saying, 'I want to come, please remember to inform us!'*"[14]

Construction of four pillars, 1972, that are to carry the weight of the sphere

Piero explains that he was, all along, not in favour of employing a contractor to oversee the construction of the Matrimandir—in reaction to Shyamsunder (who was responsible for organizing the finances) suggesting that contractors be roped in—even writing eloquently to The Mother in November 1971 about the poetics of concreting on site:

> [...] my sentiment is still to participate in a creative work directly in contact with matter, to transform it. For me, Mother, on a concreting day, in the noise of the machinery and people, when concrete flows well-mixed in the formworks and boils above the needle vibrator, there is some poetry. And when everything is over and we feel the heat of the reacting cement that rises up through our feet, this heat goes straight to the heart!

He recalls, "*When we finished the pillars, I told Shyamsunder that we either needed to buy a lot of material, scaffolding, etc. to proceed with the work, or we needed to take on a contractor, as previously suggested by many. To my pleasant surprise, he was in favour of continuing like that, with voluntary workers. We agreed to continue as is with the Aurovilians and ashramites. He may have considered two aspects: firstly, the big amounts of money involved in appointing a contractor and secondly, the enthusiasm of the Aurovilians and ashramites. I believe that Shyamsunder was himself on the crest of this wave of enthusiasm. He told me to write to The Mother and ask her. So I wrote to her with the question, 'Should we employ a contractor or should we continue as we are?' And she replied that it should continue like that: meaning, with Aurovilians, ashramites, voluntary workers, plus local employees like carpenters etc.*"

This assurance in hand, Piero would drive every morning—on his Bullet, his leather bag slung across

his shoulder—to the Matrimandir site. For the next 20 years, he would give out the work schedule every day, pulling on with a team of dedicated Aurovilian men and women. He says, *"After the decision to go on, taken in 1972, I started to prepare the complicated drawings for the upper portion of the Matrimandir."*

The Sphere: First Slab (1973)

Construction of the actual sphere started with the erection of a steel-pipe scaffolding that reached a height of 10 m, to support the 400-tonne weight of the first slab of the sphere. Eventually, the concreting for the first slab was commenced during the peak of the monsoon season. At 7.25 p.m. on 17 November 1973, extensions of the four pillars, each signifying an aspect of the Supreme Divine Mother—Mahakali

(North: Strength), Maheshwari (South: Wisdom), Mahasaraswati (West: Perfection) and Mahalakshmi (East: Harmony)—meant to support the sphere, were completed. It was later discovered that this happened at the precise moment that The Mother left her physical body.

ABOVE
Erection of steel-pipe scaffolding on the foundation to support the weight of the first slab of the sphere

BELOW
Piero Cicionesi, Ramanathan, Alain Grandcolas, Roger Anger, 1973

Finely crafted curved shuttering detail for construction of the first slab of the bottom of the sphere, 1973

The Ribs (1974–76)

After 1974, when Roger withdrew from Auroville's Committee, Piero was left with the demanding task of producing the detailed drawings required for the high quality and technological perfection of the Matrimandir, as well as supervising the daily construction crew on site. During January–February 1974, Piero and the Aurovilian community proceeded with preparations for concreting the first layers of the four ribs that would form the framework of the sphere. Gloria recalls that the casting of the second level slab was completed sometime in March.

By the beginning of 1975, work on the ribs at all four pillars had reached the halfway point after a steady succession of concreting. At 29 m above ground level the final ring beam was cast to support the roof of the Inner Chamber, in a two-day concreting job at the end of May 1976.

Piero recalls how the pipe scaffolding was meticulously taken down in June 1976. The entire community was overjoyed to see the free interior space of the Matrimandir for the first time, without the scaffolding and supports.

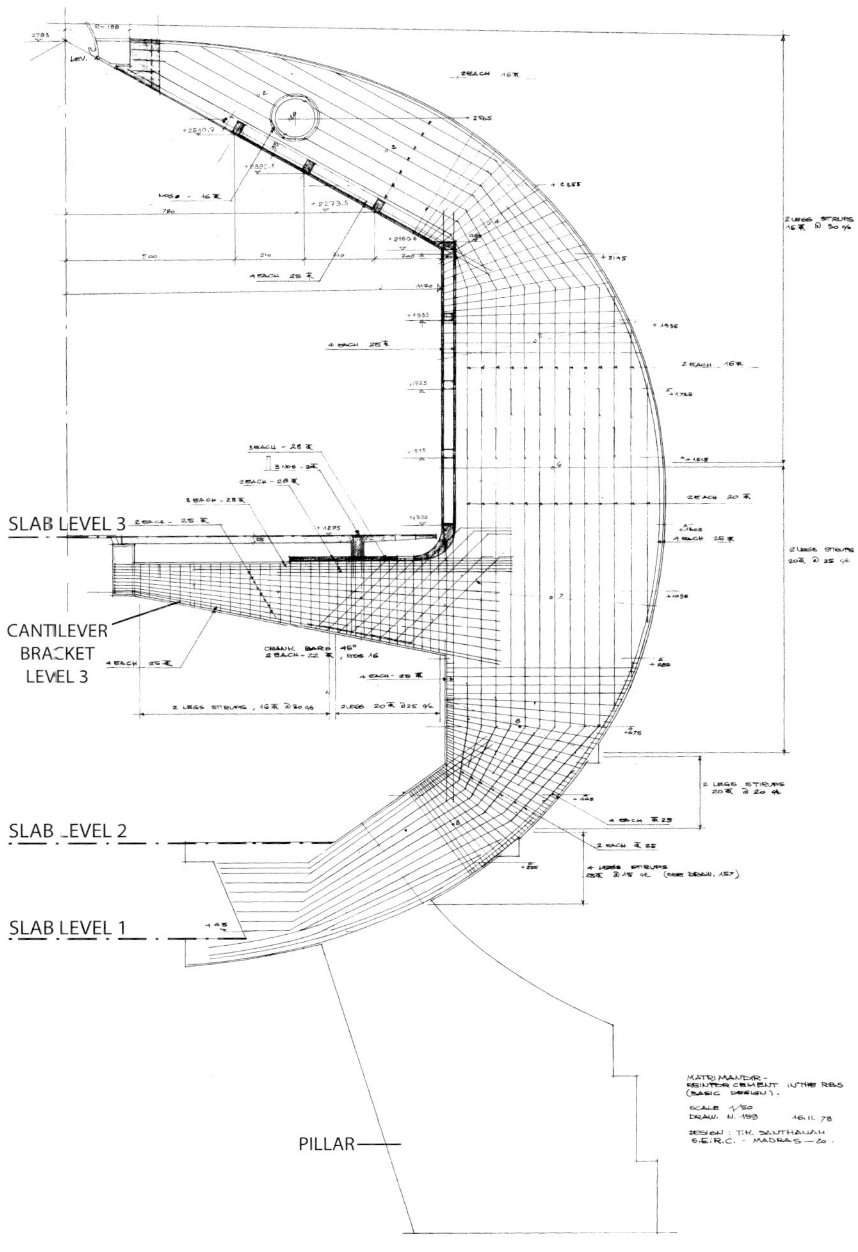

Structural drawing of a rib, by Piero

Gerard Marechal and a young Tamil boy, Ram, at the construction of the ribs

Main supporting structure of ribs completed, May 1976. Ring beams connect the arm-brackets extending from the ribs.

ABOVE
Construction of the ribs completed in 1976

BELOW
Wooden scaffolding and temporary towers for hoisting had to be erected on the four pillars.

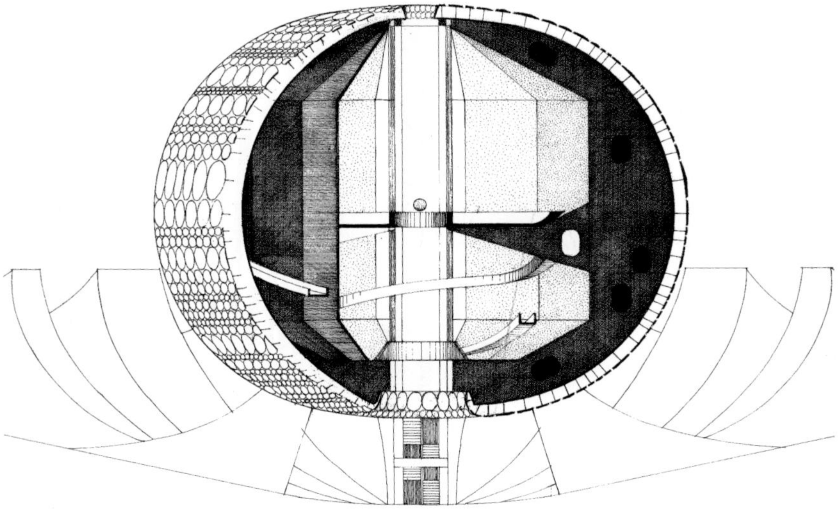

Earlier section of the Matrimandir showing the dodecagonal walls of the Inner Chamber continuing downwards, containing the ramps inside them. The drawing by Andre Hababou also shows the original pattern of discs of varying sizes on the external facade.

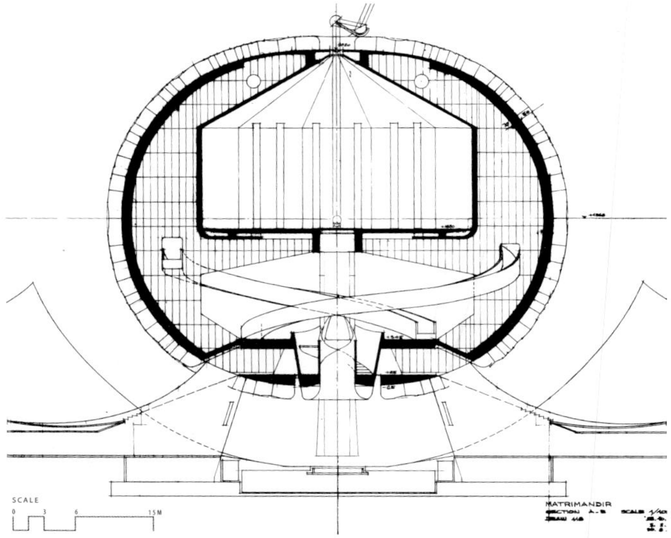

Section of the Matrimandir, 1972, showing the Inner Chamber limited to the upper portion of the globe, with the lower part dedicated mainly for the ramps, as proposed by Piero. Roger agreed to remove the lower walls of the chamber as this would free up the view of the sphere from inside.

FACING PAGE
Completed floor slab and walls of Inner Chamber, and helical ramps

Structure of the Inner Chamber (1976–79)

In November 1976, the concreting of the floor of the Inner Chamber was completed, and the work on its walls began. These were poured in layers using a specially designed and fabricated steel shuttering.

In Roger's original project, the dodecagonal wall of the Inner Chamber was extended for the full height of the sphere and the ramps were inside the Inner Chamber. Gloria remarks that it was "*taking away all the beauty of the space of the sphere*"[12] and that the staircase landing in the middle of the Inner Chamber would bring noise into it. Piero says, "*I proposed to Roger to cut off the walls [of the Inner Chamber that were extended below] so as to see the curve of the outer sphere gently going up, and he readily agreed. It was quite amazing how fast things developed at the time, and I think he never regretted those changes. It is much more interesting from inside to see the sphere than to see some concrete walls.*

"While verifying the feasibility of the structure, the engineers opposed the construction of 4 ramps that were crossing too many times the RCC ribs, making them weak... I thought of the possibility of a new solution: to make only two ramps arriving directly at the level of the entrance doors (as they are now) and to make the Inner Chamber limited to the upper portion

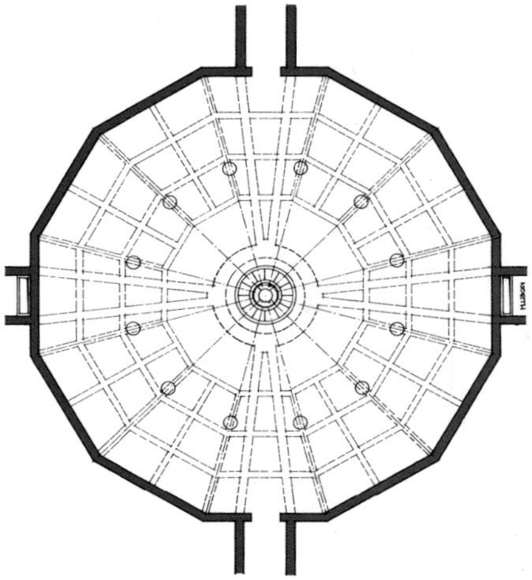

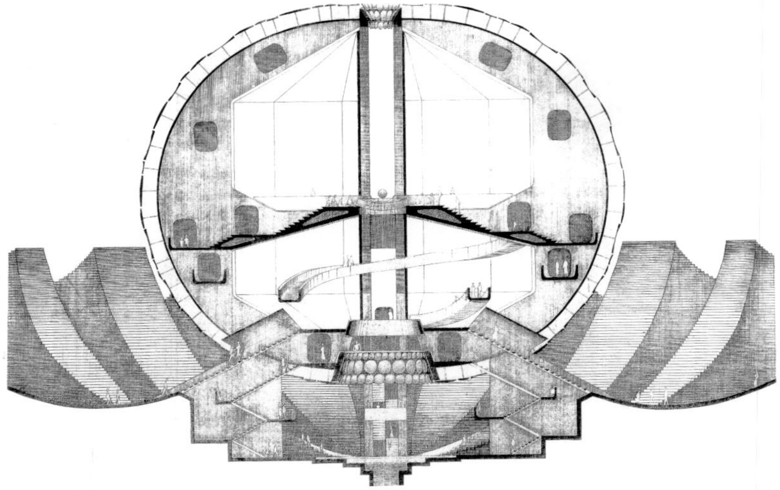

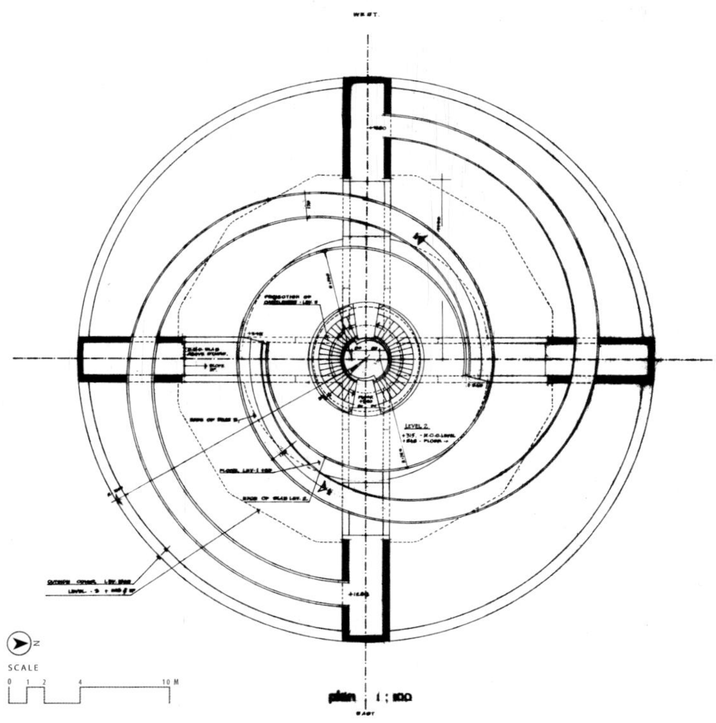

of the sphere, clearly separated from the rest. The lower part was to remain mainly dedicated to the ramps with the advantage during ascent and descent of the full view of the rising majestic geometrical surface of the sphere. I felt that, with this new solution, we were moving closer to the simple design that The Mother wanted." Both these major decisions where Piero played a pivotal architectural role were to have a major impact in the experience of the visitor to the Inner Chamber. The experience of the interior space of the sphere is heightened as one ascends the helical ramps.

Steel girder elements for the ramps that would join the second level to the Inner Chamber began to be fabricated in sections in the Matrimandir workshop. These workshops had begun as small huts to store tools but gradually became full-fledged workshops that supported the construction of the Matrimandir at every level. Neatly organized over the years, they still cater to the maintenance of the Matrimandir and execution of the gardens.

ABOVE

Volunteers carrying steel girder supports for the ramp, fabricated in the Matrimandir workshop under Piero's supervision.

BELOW

Completed structure of the Inner Chamber supported by ribs, 1979

FACING PAGE

ABOVE LEFT

Plan of the Inner Chamber showing reflected ceiling

ABOVE RIGHT

An earlier section design of the Matrimandir by Roger Anger, showing the four ramps crossing the RCC ribs many times (seen as multiple doorway punctures) and staircases ascending directly into the meditation chamber.

BELOW

Modified design with two ramps, instead of four, arriving directly at the entrance doors to the Inner Chamber.

ABOVE
Piero with engineer T.K. Santhanam, 1987

BELOW
Connection between the space frame and the ribs

FACING PAGE
The space frame 1979–87

The Space Frame (1980–87)

Recognizing the complexity of the task of creating an outer cover for the Matrimandir, Dr Chamanlal Gupta had suggested meeting structural engineers of the SERC[11] from Chennai, since they were experts in shell structures. There, Piero met a young engineer, Dr T.K. Santhanam.

The first structural option was a shell structure. After months of rigorous study, it appeared that a shell of this unusually grand size would have implied a cumbersome quantity of curved shuttering and tubular scaffolding to be kept on site for months and years. In the absence of huge sums of money, which often trickled in gradually, this would be difficult. Another option that had been considered was of a lightweight tubular structure. This idea came with its own set of problems. The use of imported corten steel was explored, but it would have been extremely expensive. Moreover, the structural design would use very different sizes of modules, with the only purpose being to follow Roger's varying disc pattern, more than to solve the static forces.

A logical solution was to deploy a concrete prefab structure made of individual components that could be cast and built incrementally in stages. Piero suggested to explore the concrete space frame proposed by Dr Santhanam, with precast elements. As Alan Lithman, alias Savitra, wrote in 1974, "Among its more material mysteries, the Matrimandir has no fixed and final architectural plan. Only the structural design has formalized and that too is subject to detail adjustments in process. It is a living and evolving form revealing itself one step at a time..."

ABOVE
Building the space frame: Piero with Patrick Dubos, 1984

BELOW
Volunteers at work, carrying precast beam elements for the space frame

Once the decision to go ahead with the pre-cast elements had been taken, Piero started refining the drawings for the outer space frame that was to give the sphere its complete form and protect the Inner Chamber from rain and sun. Describing the logic behind the design, he explains, "*The spaceframe to support the skin of the Matrimandir is a grid of triangles of varying sizes which runs the length and breadth of the sphere.*" It allows for a double skin and, though many possible materials could be used to cover the triangles of the space frame, the original plan was for ferrocement inside and 8-cm precast RCC triangles outside. However, in the end, ferrocement with portholes for light, protected by a waterproofing membrane (a coating of Kamperol), was chosen as the most adaptable material for the outer skin. Following the design conceived by Joel Koechlin, a French specialist, the inner skin was successfully done with Kevlar and fibreglass tissue (used for boat sails and ultralight aircrafts) mounted on aluminium alloy frames, following the triangular grid of the structure. This allows for a wonderful translucent and soft light to penetrate through the portholes in the ferrocement triangles.

Pre-casting of the 1,200 concrete beams that form the grid began at the end of 1979. Fitting them took eight years and was completed on 15 August 1987—Sri Aurobindo's birthday—making the space frame one of the most spectacular aspects of the structure.

Aerial photo showing the triad of Matrimandir under construction, the amphitheatre with Lotus Urn and the Banyan Tree, 1988

LEFT Community meeting, 1987, with Roger Anger (standing in centre) where it was decided that the Matrimandir would be would be covered in golden discs and not in marble or any other material like glass or copper.

RIGHT ABOVE Piero with Paolo (to his right), daughter Marta and Pascal, 1985.

RIGHT BELOW Matrimandir models in both gold disc and marble as options for Matrimandir skin, 1987

FACING PAGE Finished Inner Chamber with a ray of sunlight striking a crystal

Meanwhile, the two inner ramps were completed and the first ramp underwent a successful loading test of 20,000 kg. "*In the same year, Roger came back and was surprised by the beauty of the structure. He hugged me and told me, 'This structure is not just yours. It's coming from The Mother!' After a while, in order to follow the geometry of the space frame, he changed the pattern of the golden discs,*" says Piero. He had been a good instrument to lead such a collective effort harmoniously.

Inner Chamber Interiors (1988–91)

When Roger Anger came back to Auroville after almost a decade-long absence, a marathon community meeting lasting 10 hours was held where, after much debate, it was decided that the Matrimandir would indeed be clad in gold, as per the original design, and not in marble or any other material like glass or copper. It was a choice of the symbolism of the "sun" (gold) over the "moon" (marble). It was also decided that Piero would continue to finish the Inner Chamber and that the rest would be completed by Roger and his team. "*I appreciated that very much because I felt that he respected our previous choices and our work,*" says Piero.

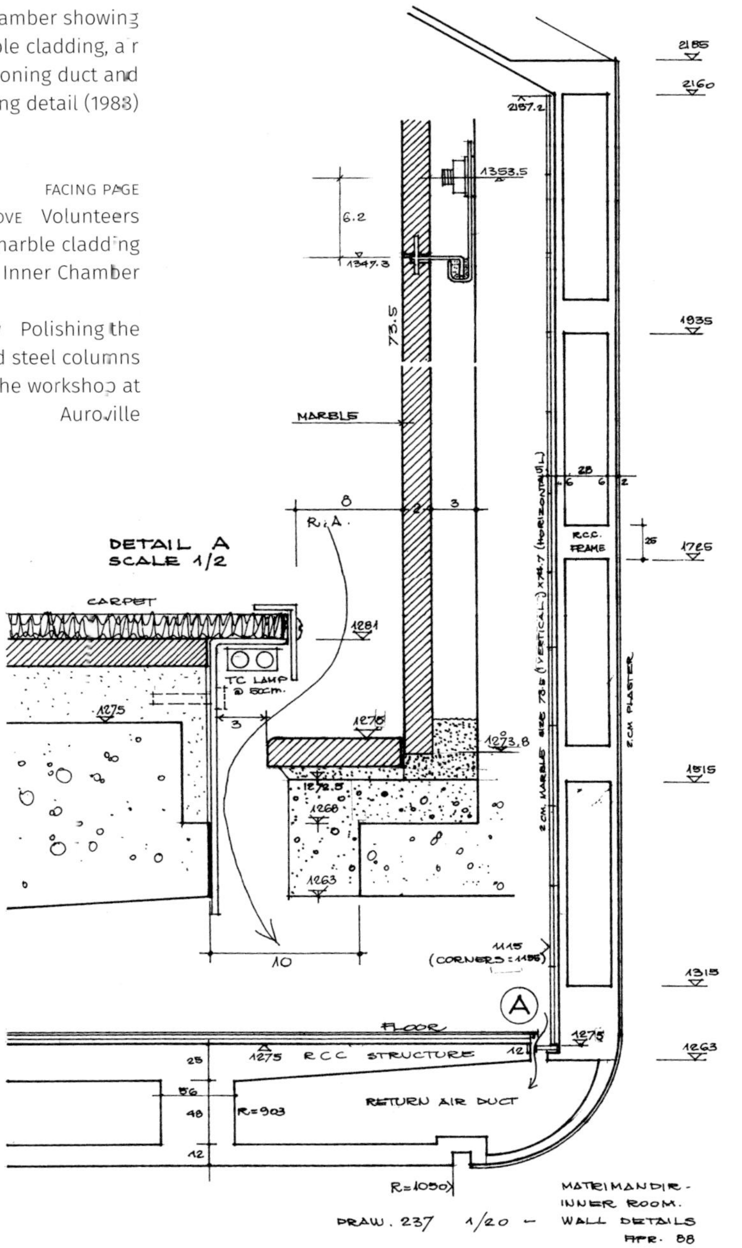

Detailed wall section of Inner Chamber showing marble cladding, air conditioning duct and flooring detail (1988)

FACING PAGE

ABOVE Volunteers mounting marble cladding in Inner Chamber

BELOW Polishing the galvanized steel columns in the workshop at Auroville

Thus the work on Inner Chamber interiors continued under the guidance of Piero. The Mother had explained her recurring vision for the inner chamber and crystal. She had said, "[The] Matrimandir... I always see it as a very big room absolutely empty. It receives light from above... the ray of light will always be there and will always strike the centre... around that people can sit and meditate, or simply rest."

Descending on to a crystal globe, the image of the sunbeam symbolized a union between spirit and matter. The Inner Chamber was a place of silence and concentration, devoid of images, since it was not a place for organized meditation or group gatherings. Piero recalls how the Inner Chamber shaped up, *"Paolo Tommasi had been the one to ask The Mother about the Matrimandir and had played a special role from the very outset. We visited him often in Pondicherry and had long discussions on the project, listening to his interpretation of her vision and of Udar's drawings. In 1973, a big model had also been presented by William Netter: an interior designer from New York. It had been a revelation about the beauty of the Inner Chamber."*

Once the decision was taken at the community meeting with Roger in 1987, Piero and team could work on the details of marble cladding, of the air conditioning ducts, of the columns, of the artificial illumination and, most importantly, of the crystal globe, the symbols that support it and the sunbeam. During the next three years of concentrated work, the Inner Chamber took shape and all the various elements found their place.

The Mother had imagined 12 columns standing in the Inner Chamber, not as structural elements but as symbolic ones. It was therefore necessary to make them very light. Gloria recalls that the size of 60-cm diameter was not suitable for aluminium. Steel tubes, as they were available in India at the time, had aesthetically unappealing welding joint all along. Piero found in Italy one of the few factories producing suitable seamless welded tubes in galvanized steel of 60-cm diameter. In 1990, they were purchased, cut to the required length, zinc-coated and imported. They were given a lengthy treatment in the Matrimandir workshop to transform them into the perfectly white matte finish desired. For this, special equipment had been designed and a team had been put together who worked on them tirelessly for years.

In the year 1977, the marble industry in India had not yet developed. The chamber walls needed more than 1,100 slabs of pure white marble. Piero visited Italy with Madanlal Himatsingka, a businessman who was a devotee and funded many of the Matrimandir's activities, and had them specifically extracted from the mountain caves of Lasa, near Bolzano in northern Italy, deep in the Alps. In hindsight, it was a timely choice since prices of marble skyrocketed in the coming years. Stored underground in the amphitheatre for several years, it finally started to be mounted on the walls of the Inner Chamber. The team working for years on the structure of the Matrimandir saw with emotion the colour of the lower reaches of the 12-sided Inner Chamber slowly changing from cement grey to dazzling white.

Although initially Piero did not think it necessary to use marble for the flooring of the chamber, since the floor was to be covered by a carpet, a devout ashramite passionately stated, *"I have marble even on my kitchen platform. We should have it at least on the*

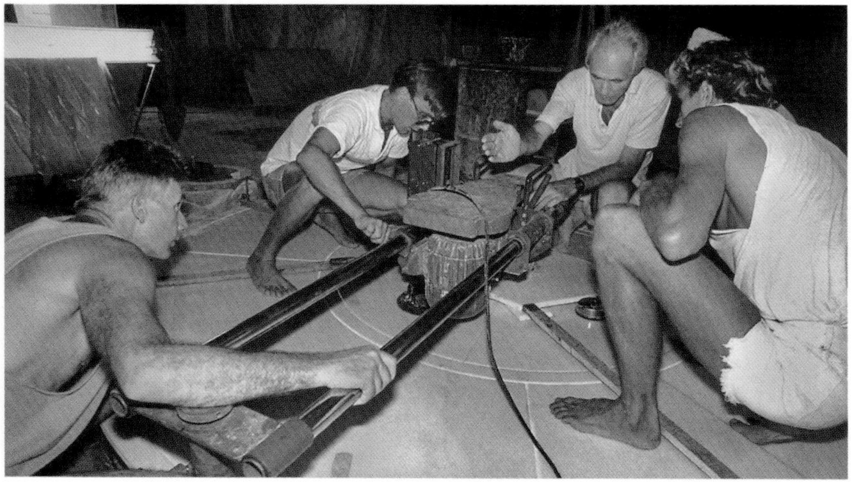

Piero with (clockwise from left) Christopher Grey, Andy Martens and Edzard Loesing carving The Mother's symbol in marble flooring of the Inner Chamber

floor of the Inner Chamber too!" This lady proceeded to fund the purchase of Makrana marble from Rajasthan. A white carpet for the Inner Chamber's floor was made in Calcutta with imported wool and with minimum joints, over a period of six months.

A special machine was made in Auroville workshops to engrave The Mother's symbol in marble of 3 m diameter. on which four of Sri Aurobindo's symbols—standing upright and joined together at the corners—would support the crystal globe of 70 cm diameter. The gilded symbols rest on the floor which has a small hole. A second lens in the slab refocuses the light beam so that it becomes visible in a lotus pool under the Matrimandir.

The air conditioning work was another facet that challenged Piero's skill in handling things to perfection. As in many aspects in the realization of the Matrimandir, the right "expert" appeared in Auroville at the right time. By the mid-eighties, ecological awareness about using Freon-based ACs had grown and Aurovilians wanted to try air conditioning the chamber (which was a necessity due to lack of openings) with solar power. A visiting Israeli engineer came and informed Piero about such an experiment that was underway in Israel. On his next visit to Rome, Piero took a flight to see this solar AC plant but sensed that it wasn't the solution for India's tropical climate and needed too much attention to run. He then tried an ammonia-based cooling option. Immediately, there was hue and cry among Aurovilians about its hazards and health effects.

Due to unreliable supply of electricity in Auroville in those days, a water-cooled system was worked out with a specialist from Chennai, Mr Kumarakrishnan. This worked for a few years. When electricity supply became steadier, this was replaced with a simpler system designed by Vladimir, a Russian Aurovilian who had recently joined the team at the Matrimandir. He reworked the entire system, employing advanced technology, and installed the noisy compressors in the ribs itself yet keeping the chamber silent as ever. *"A miracle,"* says Piero.

Crystal Globe

One of the most important elements, the raison d'être of the Matrimandir, remains the crystal globe that The Mother described as the central element in her vision of the Inner Chamber. The "crystal" globe of diameter 70 cm, the only one of its kind, is the biggest optically perfect glass globe ever made in the world.

"Nobody wanted to make a globe so big," recalls Gloria.[12] Carel Thieme, a fellow Aurovilian, enquired with Schott, a reputed glass factory in Germany specializing in optical glasses that was a direct subsidiary of Zeiss, the company famous for its big

optics in astronomy. They found the project worthy of interest. Piero and a team went together to procure the crystal from Zeiss–Schott in Germany around 1985. Gloria recollects that the crystal took a long time to make without any flaws in it, requiring months merely to cool down slowly such that it would not break, and being polished for another nine months at the Carl Zeiss AG, Germany.

Recounting his impressions on The Mother's vision of light, Piero explains, *"I found it absolutely astonishing: the extraordinary invention of the ray of the sun [sic]. How could The Mother see something like that? Where does it come from? In a way, it is a stroke of genius. A symbol, not only a physical thing, which is made out of light. The ray is alive. She said, 'I don't know exactly on what the ray is striking, and then… I have seen, I have seen! It is a globe.' She formulated that in 15 days! That has always given me an immense curiosity and a lot of energy How to make this ray happen? What are the means to do it? It is something that is not of this world,*

ABOVE
Delivery of the globe at Carl Zeiss AG, Germany, June 1988

BELOW
Piero fixing Sri Aurobindo's symbol, 1990

ABOVE LEFT
Carel Thieme, Roger Anger, Piero and Gloria studying a model of the crystal globe on Sri Aurobindo's symbol, 1988

ABOVE RIGHT
Piero, John Harper, Narayan, Adhara, Ayyanar and others fixing Sri Aurobindos' symbol in the Inner Chamber, 1992

BELOW
Andy Martens, John Harper, Adhara and volunteers finally placing the 500-kg crystal globe on Sri Aurobindo's symbol, 1992

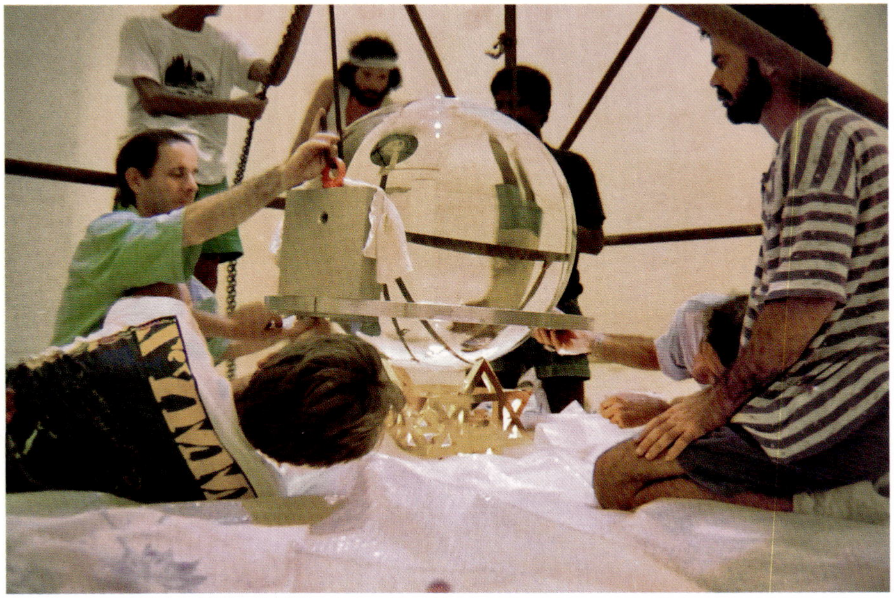

that does not belong here. Even today, I find it so mysterious. This symbol is not defined: it is a ray the globe is transparent. The symbol exists only if the ray strikes it."[14]

The Heliostat

A device to track the sun and project a beam of sunlight onto the crystal globe inside the Inner Chamber had to be devised using a mirror. Gloria elaborates on how challenging a task it proved to realize this inspired vision. "*The sun changes every day, every season, every year also! So Piero had to know how to automatically move [the heliostat's mirror] with the sun. It was very interesting for him. He just went deep inside that.*"[12] Once again, Piero's mathematical talents came to the fore.

Piero describes, "*I started to search on [sic] the heliostat in 1981. On the occasion of a visit to the United States, I visited possible installations, hoping to find a good one 'readymade' to be purchased. I came to know that a small company in New Mexico had installed one heliostat on the roof of the Hyatt Hotel in Chicago to send a bundle of sunrays into the reception area, about 50 m down. I went there to see. Nothing! With some effort, I found out that, yes, the machine was installed three years ago but removed very soon after because the ray was not stable. It was creating too many problems, including complaints from apartments on the other side of the road, that were casually receiving the ray in their windows! Discouraged, on my return to Auroville I decided to start building in our workshop a simple prototype. I studied astronomy to get information on the movement of the sun in the sky and received help from Aurelec*[15] *to start programming the complex calculations on a computer. The effort ended with a rudimental heliostat that was decently*

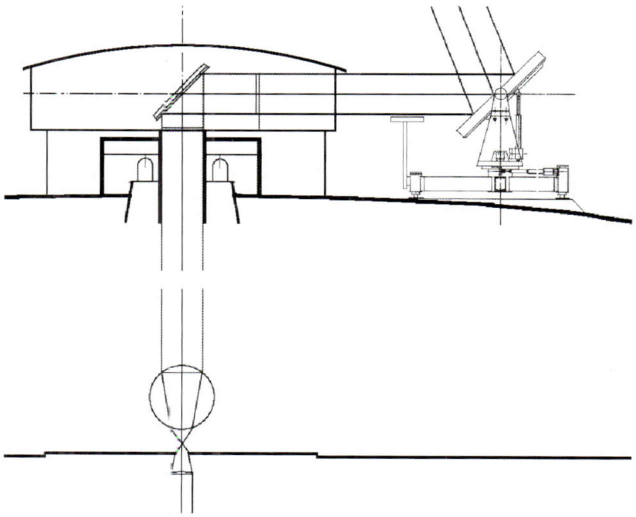

ABOVE
Piero working on the heliostat prototype

BELOW
Final drawing of heliostat by Piero

LEFT
Piero with engineer Dr Santhanam on top of the Matrimandir with the first heliostat prototype
Enhanced with BooksPlus

RIGHT
The heliostat installed on the Matrimandir, 2005

FACING PAGE
Crystal globe with Sri Aurobindo's symbol, as seen in the Inner chamber when a cloud passes overhead

tracking the sun. But its precision was not enough for our purpose.

"Next time I was in Italy, I found myself climbing the hill of Arcetri, near Florence, where Galileo had lived and studied in seclusion in his last years. There I found out from a sympathetic technician in the Solar Observatory that was nested between olive trees on top of the same hill, how they work with their telescopes. Mr Bassanese revealed to me the magic of the '2 axis pointer'. It is the same technology that is used for guiding rockets, a simplified version of which we are using in [the] Matrimandir even today!"

The heliostat was carefully fabricated, on the basis of Piero's design, by Auro Engineering, a highly specialized mechanical workshop connected with the Ashram, as an offering. The heliostat's components were ready for assembly in September 1993. The amount of light and heat on the crystal globe was studied by the engineers at Zeiss. Tests with the new heliostat were carried out to satisfaction by August 1994. In May the next year, a lens of diameter 45 cm and with focal length of 30 m, manufactured in India by General Optics (Asia) Ltd, was installed on top of the Inner Chamber to focus the sun's rays in a converging beam that would strike the globe inside the chamber.

In 1991, the crystal was finally installed. It was hoisted in a wooden crate with a plexiglas top, visible to all, and on 15 August that year—Sri Aurobindo's birthday and India's Independence Day—the Inner Chamber was opened. "*What was for me the most touching thing was that when the sky had some clouds passing by, the ray of sun made a different light on the globe,*" muses Gloria. "*It becomes so alive as if the globe is alive!*"[12]

Reflections

Roger Anger once said, "If Piero had not been there, it would never have been possible to have this kind of collective participation of Aurovilians in the building of [the] Matrimandir to such perfection."[16] Piero had had a committed team working with him for years on end, though from time to time the collective nature of the project necessitated that the community question every step and sometimes interfere, claiming "better ideas" or stir up oppositions. This often cost him much time and tried his patience.

With the installation of the crystal globe and the completion of the Inner Chamber, he felt that his role in the manifestation of the Matrimandir had been accomplished and, after more than 20 years, he withdrew from his daily visits to the site.

The Matrimandir was completed in 2008. Since then, Piero has been visiting the Inner Chamber and, more often, the gardens. Having been involved in the construction of the edifice, Piero experiences this manifestation of The Mother's vision of "the soul of Auroville" very differently. *"It will take many years for me to absorb its profound meaning and significance,"* explains Piero.

"Often I am asked if I spoke with The Mother about the Matrimandir," he says. *"On 3 April 1973, it was my birthday. I had an appointment with The Mother as in the previous years and, in spite of the difficulties of communication with her, I wanted strongly to get some clarity on the Matrimandir and my role in it! I went there and waited at length on the terrace, but she didn't receive anybody. She was not well and, from the day before, she had stopped receiving people. So the answer is I never spoke to her directly about the Matrimandir! But occasionally I wrote to her and informed her about the progress of the work. Once I even sent her a cube of concrete! Sometimes I received a nice answer. Most of the time, I received some flowers and her blessings."*

Piero introspects on the surreal process of building such a structure that emerges from the ground: *"The*

LEFT
Piero and Gloria on the Matrimandir construction site

RIGHT
Roger working on a model with a new pattern of placing gold discs on the outer skin, 1988

FACING PAGE
Matrimandir excavation scaffolding being put up at night, as the extreme heat during the day would make it difficult to handle the heated metal pipes. Piero, on top right corner, working with the team, 1973.

construction of [the]Matrimandir created a very strange situation for me because I felt that somehow I was protecting the vision of The Mother as if she was a poor lady sitting there who did not have the means of going and seeing by herself! I was helping to realize her vision the way she had seen it, against worldly forces of other people. I should have asked her for protection, and there was (instead) this feeling that I was protecting her. As if it was my duty... In effect, the physical experience to go and see The Mother was not the strongest element, for me. Once I tried to show her my drawings, I put them on her lap, but then I realized she could not see. Once Roger told me, 'When you have drawn a project, ask The Mother for her blessing, and once you have the blessings nobody will tell you anything. It is like the official seal.' [Laughs] So when we made the plans for the Health Centre, I went with my drawings, and I asked her blessings for this project. I gave her the paper and she said, 'Where is the North?' She turned the plan so that the North was on top. Then she said, 'You want my blessings?' [mischievous wink] with an air of complicity [laughs].

"I would have liked a closer relation with The Mother, but it never happened. And after all, she only had that with a few selected people. But this feeling of protecting her was much stronger than the rest of my feelings, much stronger."[14] Piero reflects further, *"I regret that I had not written on a more personal basis and I never got a more personal message from The Mother. It*

Instalment of gold discs and construction of Petals in RCC frame, ferrocement and earth filling, to be clad in red sandstone to merge with the red earth of Auroville and contrast with the green gardens and golden sphere, 1998.

FACING PAGE
Lotus pond below the Matrimandir that receives a beam of sunlight on a small crystal, 2008

would have been a big push for me to receive a sort of personal message, one of those short lines that she used to write. I would have liked to know... Is this my real destiny? For whom am I doing this work on the Matrimandir? For The Mother, for the Divine, for Roger? I understood I was working for Auroville."

And the Work Goes On

After 1987, architect Roger Anger had started to follow consistently and directly on-site design and construction of the rest of the works, with hundreds of different details finalized and executed by a team under his supervision.

The outer skin was to be covered by decorative, gold-leafed, concave and convex discs, mounted onto the structure by a system of metal rods. They would have the practical function of shading the building from the strong sunlight of the tropics. Although they felt that it was a high-maintenance choice, Piero and Gloria did not oppose this decision. After several years of trials, a first series of discs was made in polyester, most of which were replaced by stainless steel discs.

In August 1995, gilding of the discs began under the guidance of a master gilder from France. About 461 big convex discs (diameter: 2.3 m) and 954 small (diameter: 1.4 m) concave discs were to be produced. After years of research in Asia and Europe, a method was chosen to encase the gold leaf between two thin layers of glass, sealed at the edges, to yield a 4x4 cm gold tile. It offered a solution that answers not only requirements of durability but also of easy maintenance. The gold would be safe inside the glass which could be scrubbed, brushed and sprayed. Replacement of one or more of the gold tiles could

Satellite image showing the peripheral pathway around the Matrimandir gardens in the shape of a *shaligram* 10 times bigger than the Matrimandir's outline. One can see that the east-west axis is rotated by 5 degrees anticlockwise, decided by the sun's position on 4th April, the day Sri Aurobindo arrived in Pondicherry in 1910.

also be done easily. By December 2000, 852 golden discs were mounted on the structure's skin.

Simultaneously the work on the 12 "petals" started, symbolizing the emerging of the sphere from the earth, a breaking of a new Force from Matter. This gives a dynamic upward surge to the built-form, creating an enclosure to the lower hemisphere, conducive to the original vision of a descent into earth and then an ascending approach to the Inner Chamber: a passage to initiation. The petals are clad in red sandstone from Rajasthan and hold within their ribbed RCC structure enclosed with ferrocement and earth, 12 meditation rooms, each shaped like an egg and each in a different colour with different spherical objects of light.[17]

A "lotus pond" below the Matrimandir receives a beam of sunlight directed from the top of the Matrimandir to the bottom. Roger created 216 stylized petal-shaped marble slabs here as a pond, at the centre of which is a small crystal that receives this light.

Currently in progress, the 12 gardens[18] surrounding the Matrimandir finish the whole ensemble creating a Zone of Peace at the heart of Auroville. When completed, the sky, water and earth shall come together here in a harmonious whole.

It is unfortunate that Roger passed away just a month before the final inauguration. He always maintained that the Matrimandir was the result of team work and belongs to humanity as a whole, as a symbol. From the outset, Roger had evolved an active and deep collaboration in various stages of the Matrimandir's construction. The involvement of Paolo Tommasi, Charles Gianferrari, Piero Cicionesi, T.K. Santhanam, Jacqueline Lacoste, Michael Bonke and Joel Koechlin, along with the tireless dedication and effort of the Auroville community, eventually enabled this project to be realized.

Every part of the Matrimandir has been carried out with conviction and passion. It stands as testimony, not only to The Mother's vision but also to the fact that it is indeed possible to build such a grandiose and iconic building as team work, as an intuitive, fluid and collective aspiration—without organized schedules, management consultants, contracting agencies or cost estimates—and yet achieve perfection in matter.

Notes

1. Alan Lithman (Savitra), *Auroville: Sun Word Rising* (Auroville: Community of Auroville, 1980 [1st Edition]).
2. G. Gilles, "Matrimandir - The Soul of Auroville, Book 2: Architecture and Symbolism," March 2009.
3. The "Park of Unity" would consist of 12 gardens representing the "12 attributes of the Universal Mother", surrounded by a lake. An American horticulturist, Narad, was called by The Mother to initiate the work on the Matrimandir Gardens. She said, "It must be a thing of great beauty, of such beauty that when people come they will say 'Ah, this is it!' It must be an expression of that consciousness which we are trying to bring down. One must know how to move from consciousness to consciousnesses." In early 1963, The Mother gave the names to the Matrimandir's 12 gardens: Existence, Consciousness, Bliss, Light, Life, Power, Wealth, Utility, Progress, Youth, Harmony, Perfection.
4. "The Matrimandir will be the soul of Auroville. The sooner it is there, the better it will be for everybody and especially for the Aurovilians." Words of The Mother, 15 November 1970.
5. "Tamas", in Hindu philosophy, means darkness, representing disorder, chaos, apathy, lethargy, violence and ignorance.
6. G. Gilles, "Matrimandir - The Soul of Auroville, Book 2: Architecture and Symbolism," March 2009.
7. These conversations were later published in *Mother's Agenda*, a set of 13 volumes of recorded talks with disciple Satprem. Published by Institut de Recherches Evolutives, Paris, 1976 onwards.
8. Roger adopted the Shaligram from the book of Ajit Mookerjee, *Tantra Art* (Ravi Kumar, 1967). Tantric tradition states that the creation, or matter, is contained in, and has issued forth from, this "egg".
9. See architecture diploma thesis: "Form, structure, energy – A study of the Great Pyramid and Matrimandir" by Mona Doctor (CEPT, 1990).
10. "Navoditte remembers", taken from "Matrimandir excavation 40 years ago," *Auroville Today*, no. 262 (April 2011).
11. Structural Engineering Research Centre, Chennai, is recognized as a leading research institution in the field of structural engineering, nationally and internationally. It is one of the national laboratories under the Council of Scientific and Industrial Research, India.
12. Francois Gautier video, "Gloria - serving the construction of the Matrimandir".
13. Chetties are metal containers used to carry material during construction.
14. Excerpted partially from a conversation with Christine: "Turning Points," *Auroville Press*, May 2009.
15. Aurelec was Auroville's biggest computer hardware companies in the early eighties.
16. In a personal interview with Mona Doctor-Pingel and Anupama Kundoo in 2006.
17. "The 12 petals [of The Mother's symbol] signify anything one wants, you see. That's the number of Aditi, of Mahashakti, so it applies to everything: all her actions have 12 aspects. There are also Her 12 virtues, 12 powers, 12 aspects. And then Her 12 planes of manifestation and many other things that are 12… it is the symbol of manifestation, double perfection in essence and in manifestation, in the Creation." Explanation of The Mother to her class in 1954. The 12 meditation rooms in the petals represent the 12 virtues or qualities: sincerity, humility, gratitude, perseverance, aspiration, receptivity, progress, courage, goodness, generosity, equality, peace. Each of these qualities was assigned a corresponding colour by The Mother.
18. The path that surrounds the periphery of the garden is also in the shape of a Shaligram 10 times bigger than the section of Matrimandir. Roger once told The Mother that this had happened without conscious intention, to which she responded that the number 10 signifies accomplishment. For more on the gardens, see Note 3.

Divine Workers

Dr Chamanlal Gupta

I have known Piero since he and Gloria arrived at Auroville in March 1968, as a professional of highest competence and integrity, and as a friend. Gloria, an equally accomplished architect, has stood beside Piero, best expressed in the words of Sister Nivedita,[1] "as quiet and warm as sunshine", luminous and not a shadow.

Piero has an almost unequalled mastery of detailing, limitless capacity for work and endurance. In obedience to The Mother's command to make the Matrimandir a strong and durable structure, he practically relinquished his architectural practice to become a construction engineer, a job that he did day and night for over 20 years with unflagging zeal and dedication. He learnt concrete technology, structural engineering, air conditioning, astronomy, solar optics, soil engineering from basic text books, as required for his work. He earned the incredulous looks of allied consultants at the beginning and, later, admiration for his thoroughness and mastery. Sri Aurobindo Ashram's chief engineer, Vishwanath, an equally good learner, who learnt German and computer programming at 80 plus, once said to me: "Piero is not only an architect and an engineer but a true yogi, for otherwise he could not have achieved the perfection he has achieved." Once, I suggested to Piero to write a

Airplane hangars in Orbetello, Italy, by Pier Luigi Nervi, 1941

Around 1974–75, in order to reduce the general weight of the structure and yet to maintain the structural depth required by the calculations, Dr Santhanam proposed to design the curved RCC space frame of Matrimandir as a grid of binary beams. Years later, it was discovered that Pier Luigi Nervi had adopted a similar, elegant binary-beam space frame structure for an airplane hangar built between 1938–1941 in Orbetello, Italy. Unfortunately, that structure was completely destroyed a few years later during the Second World War.

book. He said, *"I will bend more bars and mix more concrete for the Matrimandir than waste time writing a book."* And right enough, we have seen him supervising the Matrimandir concreting, practically each of the times, and once for more than 50 hours. This book finally pays tribute to their lifelong dedication to Auroville.

Late Professor G.S. Ramaswamy, a renowned structural engineer and a student of Timoshenko and Director of Structural Engineering Research Centre, Chennai[2] (the structural design consultants for Matrimandir), came to Auroville and visited the Matrimandir with Piero. After asking a few questions, he remarked, "Mr Cicionesi, you can be proud of what you have achieved. I have never seen such quality of concrete. You are truly Nervi of India." I saw Piero's face melting and eyes moistening. Later, Gloria unfolded the mystery by telling that Nervi was Piero's hero during his architectural studies. A world-class Indian structural engineer telling an Italian architect that he was India's Nervi can only happen in Auroville.

Later, when Dr O.P. Jain—Director of IIT[3] Delhi, a great structural engineer, and chairman of Research Advisory Committee of SERC—visited the Matrimandir, he asked Piero how he anchored such heavy marble doors of the Matrimandir chamber such that they swing freely like a leaf. Piero explained to him all the details and said that this was the result of very good team work in Auroville. Dr O.P. Jain said it must be so because unless he had seen what he just saw, he would not have believed that it was possible at all.

The consultants, Mr Natarajan for structures, Mr Kumarakrishnan for air conditioning, engineers of General Optics for solar optics, and all others were truly astonished by Piero's knowledge in spite of serious professional differences at the beginning.

The Matrimandir was completed in 2008. After my 75th birthday meditation in the Inner Chamber, I spontaneously went to meet Piero because I had not seen him for some time. When I wanted to know about his feelings about the Matrimandir, he took my breath away. He said, *"Chamanlalji, when I finished the Inner*

Space frame designed to support the outer cover of the Matrimandir, 1987

Piero with the marble doors during construction of the Matrimandir's Inner Chamber

FACING PAGE
Completed Matrimandir space frame, 1987

Chamber and handed over the project to Roger for finishing the rest of the building, I was a bit apprehensive about the quality of detailing. But I surrendered because my part was over. Then I saw Roger, working on it himself and on the construction site, hour after hour, day after day, in spite of his frail health, and what we have is a building of stunning beauty, which has surpassed all expectations of all of us."

Regrettably, Roger passed on to the other world just a month before the opening of the Matrimandir.

In The Mother's work, surrender, competence and dedication are the keys to receive her grace, and Piero has been a great receptacle for a marvellous manifestation. As for Gloria, she has brought sweetness, sensitivity and mellowed lines to their joint architectural projects, which might have been difficult for Piero's austere discipline to crystallize.

Notes

1. Sister Nivedita, born Margaret Elizabeth Noble (28 October 1867–13 October 1911) was a Scottish–Irish social worker, author, teacher and a disciple of the Hindu monk Swami Vivekananda.
2. CSIR–Structural Engineering Research Centre (CSIR-SERC), Chennai, India, is one of the national laboratories, started in the late sixties, under the Council of Scientific and Industrial Research (CSIR), India. CSIR–SERC has built-up excellent facilities and expertise for the analysis, design and testing of structures and structural components.
3. Indian Institute of Technology, Delhi (abbreviated IIT Delhi or IITD) is a public research university located in Delhi, India started in 1961. It was declared an Institute of National Importance by the Government of India under Institutes of Technology Act. IIT Delhi is one of the two educational institutes in India that have been listed in Quacquarelli Symonds' (QS) list of top 200 universities globally in 2015.

SELECTED WORKS

ASPIRATION HUTS

Auroville, 1969–1972

FACING PAGE

ABOVE LEFT

The first prototype at Hope Community: Roger Anger with Vincenzo Maiolini

ABOVE RIGHT

Cluster of huts under construction at Aspiration

BELOW

The first prototypes at Aspiration, made using a square brick base, 1970. The community kitchen can be seen in the background.

Rising out of the red soil, poised next to a canyon cut deep by the eroding soil, photos of "Aspiration Huts" from the early seventies are testimony to the creativity of the architect aspiring to make the maximum from the minimum—minimum resources, minimum possessions, minimum privacy—while creating optimum spaces for the sparse and simple yet rich life that early Aurovilians shared.

The genesis of the Aspiration huts lies in the experimental modules tried out by Roger Anger and his team at Promesse and Hope communities. They built upon the local *keet* (coconut leaf) huts that already existed in the surrounding villages. The idea was to explore cost-effective, modular and temporary housing with local materials and know-how, in the outlying lands of Auroville. With the impending arrival of two busloads from Paris (referred to as "caravans" in Auroville's history), Piero and Gloria were given the task to design temporary housing for them. These young, mostly French nationals, were attracted by The Charter of the young fledgling community of Auroville in 1970 enough to leave everything behind and come to India. The journey from Paris to Auroville took approximately six weeks. When the first batch of 15 arrived in October 1969, the initial 36 huts were underway. and Aspiration became a collective building site for some months. By 1974 the community housed 125 persons from five different continents.

The site chosen was near the school cluster and the community of Auromodele already started by Anger as experiments for the city that was to come. Located not far from the beach, there were hardly any trees as is evident in the early photos, with the Bay of Bengal in the east clearly seen in the background.

The layout of Aspiration shows a large playground with a community kitchen and clusters of huts with two types of base plans with pitched roofs. Piero and Gloria took the basic square hut module of the Hope community and modified it to have bigger spaces and additional functions. The first type (1969–70) consists of two squares rotated at 45 degrees and joined at their tips, lending a common triangle space for the

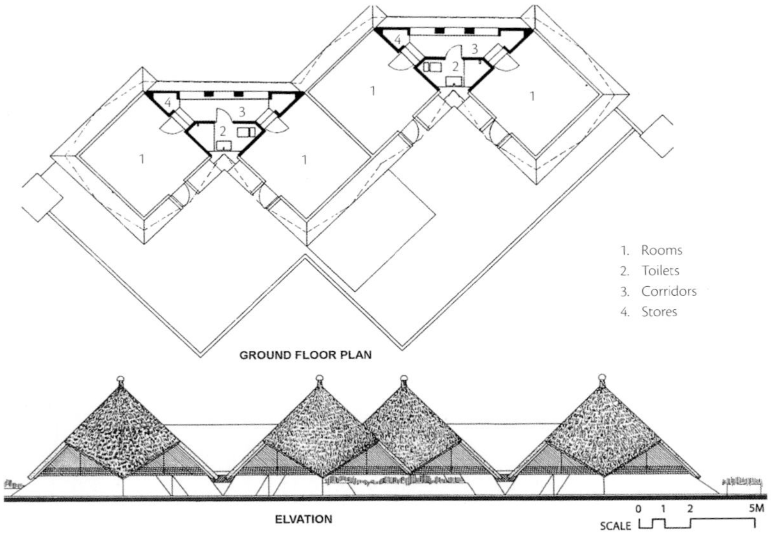

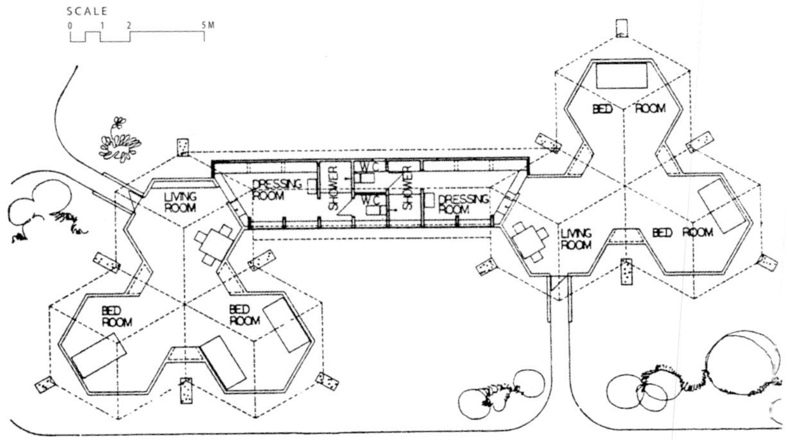

LEFT
The first prototypes were made using a square brick base, 1969. Two squares make a unit, having shared toilets. Four such modules make a cluster that is repeated.

RIGHT
Plan of prototypes with three hexagonal module, 1971–72. Each cluster was made of six such hexagonal modules and then repeated.

shared toilets and kitchenette. The roof was made of three quadrilateral frames, again rotated 45 degrees to the base, covered with coconut palm leaves and topped with rice-straw thatch, leaving triangular windows closed with plywood or cloth shutters. These were meant for single/double occupancy, each assigned a square of 16 sq. m.

The second type (1971–72) is a cluster of three hexagonal bases (approx. 50 sq. m) with the same pitched roof structure, and was designed as family units with their own personal living room, bathroom and kitchenette.

The huts were an earth-hugging low scale development. Plinth was almost non-existent. The roof hung low over the triangular windows to keep out the glaring sun and to protect from the frequent sandstorms that brought a fine layer of dust into the houses. The bathrooms were brought even lower into the ground, perhaps to facilitate easy infrastructure and to maintain the scale. A Zen-like space was created using a very sparse material palette: wooden rafters and thatch for the roof, low brick walls painted white, windows made of light flaps lined with cloth or plywood and a red oxide cement floor.

The Aspiration kitchen was designed as a community space and, over a span of 50 years, has seen many changes and varied uses. The large timber A-frame structure is dexterously designed to span 8m, with a *keet* roof. For many years, it was the hub of all social interactions in the community and the space around it was used very effectively: for theatre, kitchen gardens, children's playground and for a short time even as the planning office for Roger Anger and his team. In the turbulent times for the Sri Aurobindo Society, it became the political hotbed of Auroville.

Today, however, times have changed. Auroville has turned into a lush green forest from the barren red desert that it once was. Frequent dust storms are no more the norm. The microclimate has changed with the growing trees. The low, earth-hugging forms

ABOVE
Inside a hexagonal module hut

BELOW LEFT
Aspiration huts, Auroville, 1971

BELOW RIGHT
Aspiration community, 1972

ABOVE Interior of Aspiration kitchen/dining hall, 1974

BELOW Aspiration kitchen, detailed drawing of the timber roof construction

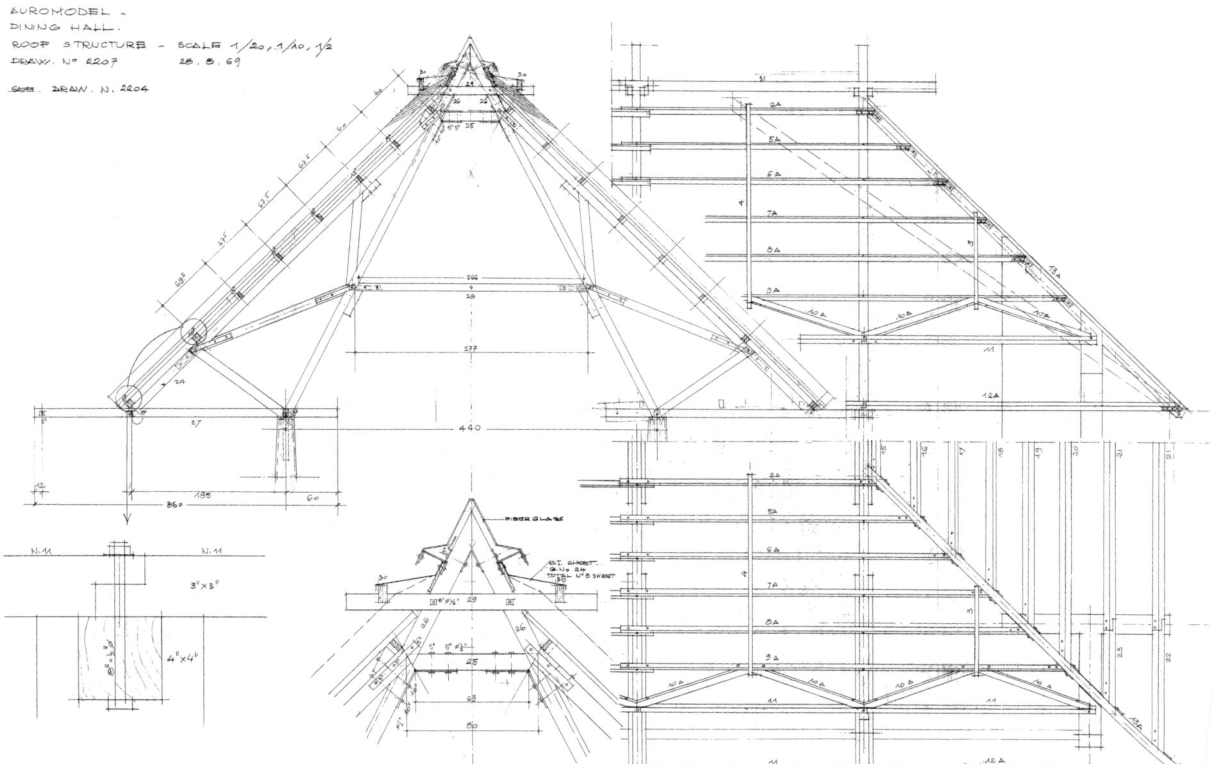

appear incongruous in the hot and humid climate that demands high plinths and good cross-ventilation. The huts have all been transformed into shapes and sizes of all kinds, with the *keet* roofs replaced with tile roofs.

Lifestyles and expectations, too, have changed. The original people who occupied the huts are all gone. They've either moved elsewhere or have left Auroville. Since there is no private ownership of property, according to the Charter of Auroville, there is a constant flux of changes in occupants of the buildings as per their needs and growth. Needs of acoustic privacy; more light and ventilation; threat of thieves; protection against crawlies and mosquitoes; and problems of rising humidity from the floor have necessarily led to major changes and consequently have destroyed the purity and simplicity of the original ensemble. Today, Piero and Gloria reminisce without nostalgia that the simple huts planned for a maximum of six months of occupancy are still in use today with all the changes

Started as a temporary community, Aspiration remains a touchstone in Auroville's history and landscape. Today, its significance is more psychological than physical, as time need not stand still for a built-form, but the associated memories live on, anchoring a collective to the place.

Aspiration huts, Auroville, 1972

Enhanced with BooksPlus

Auroson's Home

Auroville, 1969–1970

> "New words are needed to express new ideas. New forms are necessary to manifest new forces."
>
> —The Mother
>
> (1 August 1954)

A landmark in Auroville's physical evolution, Auroson's home was the first pukka individual house to be built within the proposed masterplan of Auroville. Frederick and Shyama, a young German–Swedish couple came to Pondicherry in 1966. When they felt the need to build a house of their own (a rarity in those days, when community living was the norm), as they already had three children, The Mother wrote to Frederick that it must be "a new house for a new consciousness".

Contemporaneously, Roger Anger was working on prototypes for Auroville housing, situated in the outskirts of the future city. He felt that a collective living based on compact cluster typologies should be the way forward and proposed the "mushroom houses" in 1969. However, this form with its spiral staircases, seemed impractical for a family dwelling. Frederick then approached The Mother, who directed him to Piero and Gloria, who had just arrived the year before. She said, "I see the house. Speak to them. Maybe they are receptive to get this vision."

The Mother selected a site on the edge of the proposed green belt of the masterplan, which was at the time barren, owing to its connectivity with a road leading to Pondicherry. She wished for the house to be ready in time for the birth of Frederick and Shyama's son, Auroson. This house was to be a statement—"we

East face of Auroson's Home

ABOVE Mushroom House, section by Roger Anger

BELOW View from the southeast, perspective drawing by Piero

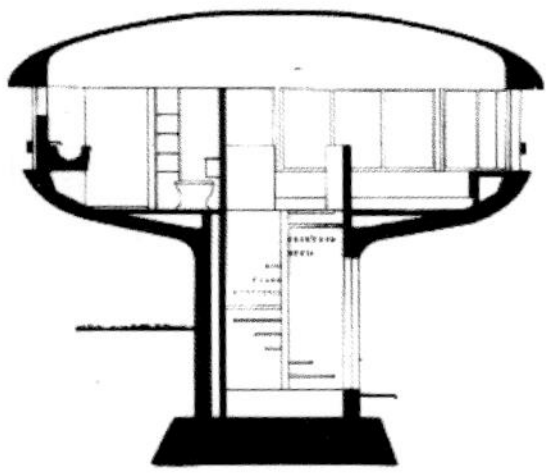

are here to stay"—and a message to be sent out to all. Indeed, Frederick lived by this "mantra" as he strove to actualize the house. When The Mother saw the first model that Piero presented, Fredrick relates that she said, "He got it." The settlement that formed around this house, in the years after, was to be named as "Certitude".

Speaking of their novel explorations in this emerging city, Piero and Gloria explain, *"After arriving in Auroville, in 1968, for many years, our main reference was the Golconde Ashram in Pondicherry. We admired the design of details by Antonin Raymond and George Nakshima, its garden, and most of all, the way it was built by voluntary workers (the* sadhaks*). In some ways, for us, in its modernity, this building was also fitting extraordinarily well with India."* Coupling some of these observations with those of traditional Tamil courtyard houses, Piero and Gloria followed the basic vocabulary of modern architecture: *"...free volumes well resting on the ground, open plan, relation with the surrounding nature, and continuity between inside and outside."* Influences from an early training in Finland are also evident in the simplicity and attention to details that characterize this work.

Explaining the process of construction, Piero says, *"During the seventies and part of the eighties, the contractors available were not skilled and refined as the ones in the big cities. They could not read the details of our drawings and, of course, the language barrier was hard to bridge. To reach a quality result in the construction we had to spend a lot of time with the masons and carpenters, explaining with samples,*

directly on the site." The clients also formed an integral part of the team and Frederick would organize the labour and purchase materials, which would be brought to the site in bullock carts.

At the time, Frederick and Shyama had idealistic notions of living in contact with nature, in a home with no walls but with a safe inner core. The design posed challenges of integrating the external world of the community, in which they were to play a pivotal role as pioneers on the land, and environment, with the internal world of the family. The sense of arrival into this house is thus a multilayered one. The southern edge, with its sliding doors, seems to embrace the community, while the northern edge has private bedrooms tucked into it, amidst a series of parallel walls. Two staggered courtyards, which bring nature into the most intimate spaces of the house, form a buffer zone between these and the shared spaces. The plan comprises two L-shaped units, each having a single storey, a courtyard and a double storey. These are designed as modules so that repetition can occur, if needed. A dynamic organization is employed, capturing the spirit of change underpinning the foundation of Auroville. As Frederick puts it, "The house is not a circle or a square. It is like a line or an arrow. [...] This house is good for leading a yogic life. [...] Spaces must shelter but not restrict one. They must give one a space to grow. A philosopher had once said that all people should be architects. And that all architects should be teachers. Most architects seem to do this by building for the 'future client', thinking that they can thereby accelerate the evolution. That the client will somehow grow into the space. How does one provide a rigid structure that still allows for evolution? Piero does so by creating depersonalized

LEFT North facade of Golconde Ashram in Pondicherry designed by Antonin Raymond and George Nakashima (1935-42), with adjustable asbestos cement louvres. Photo: 2015

RIGHT North facade of Auroson's Home, Auroville, 1970: RCC louvres as a climatic response to the harsh sunlight.

spaces—skeletons—that are beautiful in themselves. And this lends them timelessness."

LEFT A community meeting, 1980, in the double height space of the living room having a sunken floor with inbuilt seating. The elegant double stringer beam in wood echoes Leonardo Ricci's work.

The sense of arrival into the house is marked by a gradual sense of anticipation as one traverses the front yard to enter into a generous living room: a double-height space with a central wooden staircase and a sunken floor with inbuilt seating for gatherings bathed by diffused light that filters in across the louvres fixed above. The possibility of opening the wooden sliding doors into the front yard made it a special asset for the community back in the seventies, when community meetings were held here.

A porch extends towards the east. The elegant gesture of this seemingly floating heavy expanse is made possible with the use of parapet beams (inverted beams), references for which have been drawn from the works of Leonardo Ricci and Carlo Scarpa. Here, one can sit amidst the trees and the east–west breeze.

One observes, in Auroson's home, the beginnings of an architectural language that continues to evolve in the later projects of Piero and Gloria. Corners are

accentuated. Walls seem to hover over the ground. Slabs appear to float above walls. These gestures lend a sense of layered planes. Their later works are characterized by heightened attention to these particular junctions, as each element seems to strive to express its distinctiveness.

Openings are regulated by large concrete louvers, which are effectively designed to break the light, whilst retaining a sense of mass in the overall spatial form. Wide sliding doors enable openness and there is an absence of the grill-and-mosquito-net ensemble that characterizes most Auroville buildings today. All walls, sliding doors and concrete louvres, are painted white, evoking the spirit of Modernism. White masses and voids with elongated beams and walls rise out of the red soil echoing works of architect Richard Meier, and a Wrightian horizontality. Yellow tandoor stones adorn the floors. One may observe that in that early visionary phase of idealistic manifestations, one could naively overlook considerations of termites, mosquitoes, dust and thieves. Hence, the freedom with which these details were designed is evident. As Frederick and Shyama's son Auroson, who grew up in the house, aptly puts it, "This house was designed with no fears!"

View towards the east porch, with sliding doors open. A bed of pebbles marks the threshold between the built and nature.

FACING PAGE, RIGHT
The 9 x 4 m linear expanse of the dining porch, coupled with its low volume, accentuates a sense of horizontality.

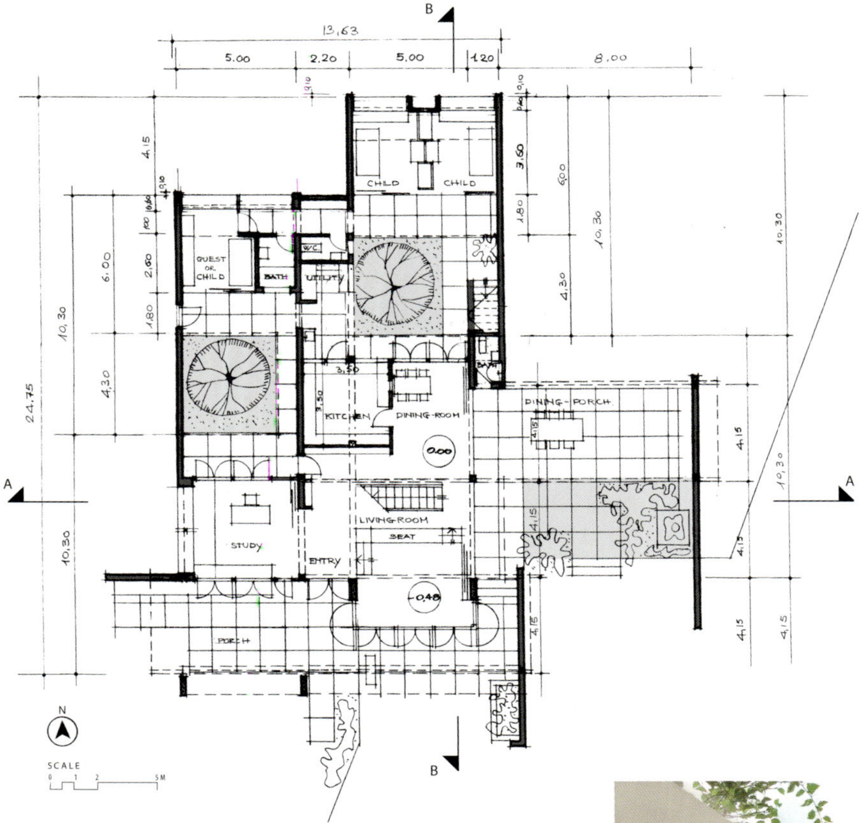

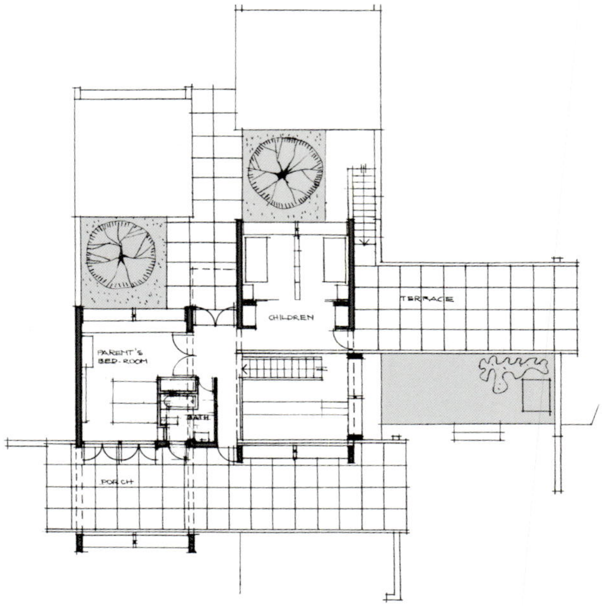

ABOVE LEFT Ground floor plan

ABOVE RIGHT First floor plan

BELOW An internal courtyard between the dining room and the children's' rooms, inspired by the local Tamil courtyard houses. This forms a buffer zone between the living space and private spaces, with a staircase ascending to the terrace.

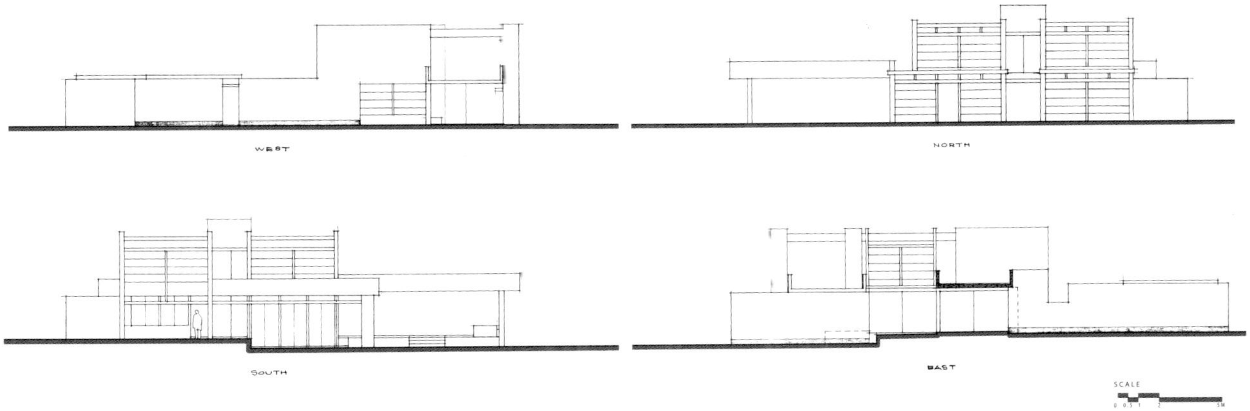

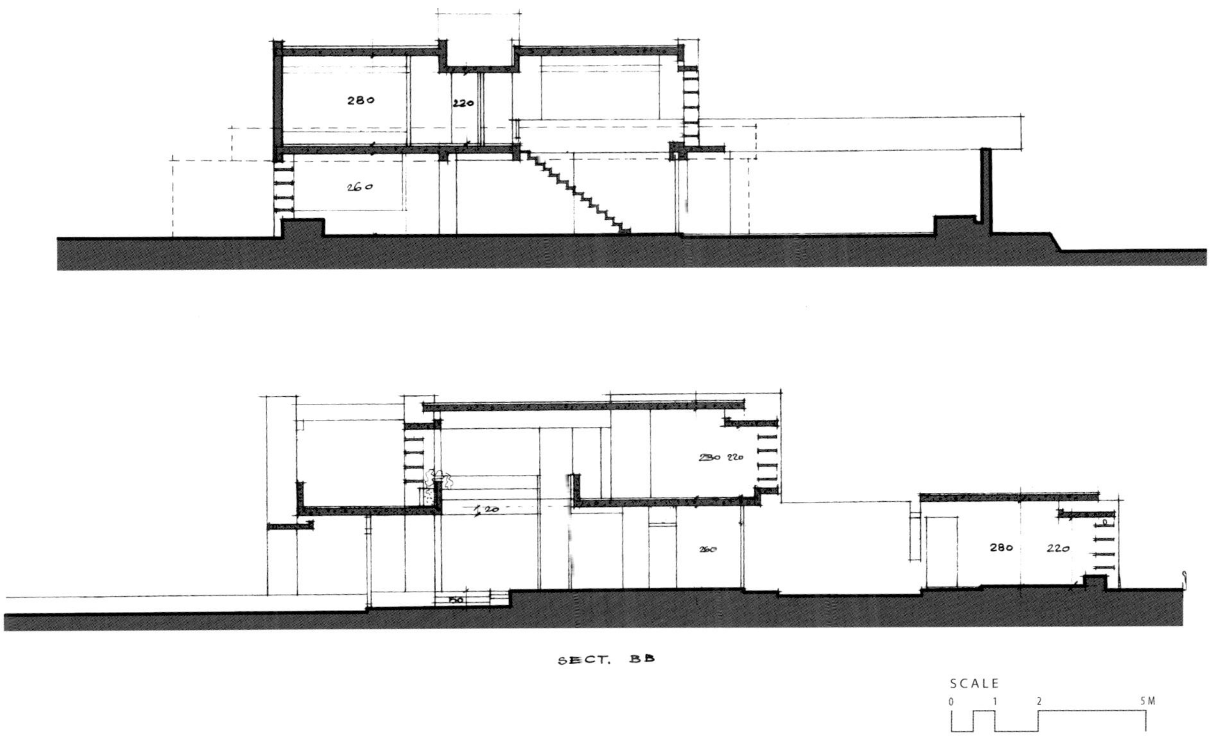

ABOVE
Elevations

BELOW
Sections

Cluster of Three Houses

Certitude, Auroville, 1972–1973

"My first impression of Auroville when I visited in the early seventies was one of utter surprise at discovering a way of life that was an experiment with frugality, reverence, togetherness, tolerance, sharing and searching for an integral way of living.

"Seeing the few buildings almost on a barren land, each shelter and cluster appeared to be building a new community where dialogue, exchange of purpose and search for constant evolution were the main thrust. I found in their discussions no worries about scarcity, only a deep-seated aspiration to minimalism and a sense of pride in discovering new ways to face the harsh and unpredictable climatic conditions. All this without expecting any monetary returns"

—B.V. Doshi[1]

The cluster of three houses in Certitude is an experiment in how arrangements of modules could facilitate collective life. While several individual houses came up in Auroville between the seventies and nineties, the creation of a sense of community has been a parallel exploration.

Piero and Gloria were also working, at the time, on the design of the Health Centre in the Aspiration community. They were sharing a studio space with Poppo Pingel, the German architect, who had also arrived in 1970 and was simultaneously working on projects such as the Fraternity Workshops and the Handmade Paper Factory. It is apparent in these projects that Roger, as the chief architect, pushed them to achieve a synthesis between their inherent aesthetic sensibilities and a dynamic form-oriented approach. Roger later told Piero that he considered the "cluster of three houses" as one of their best projects.

LEFT
Handmade paper factory by Poppo Pingel, 1973

RIGHT
Health Centre by Piero and Gloria, 1972–76

ABOVE Cluster of Three Houses, 1973

BELOW LEFT Fixed concrete louvres, a characteristic element from their other works, modulate the surface. Beams extend from columns and their ends are chamfered, giving a dynamism. Accentuated plinths allow the building to sit lightly on the earth, while ribbon windows below the ceiling make the slabs appear as if they float.

BELOW RIGHT Gloria standing in the courtyard of one of the houses, which eventually became their residence.

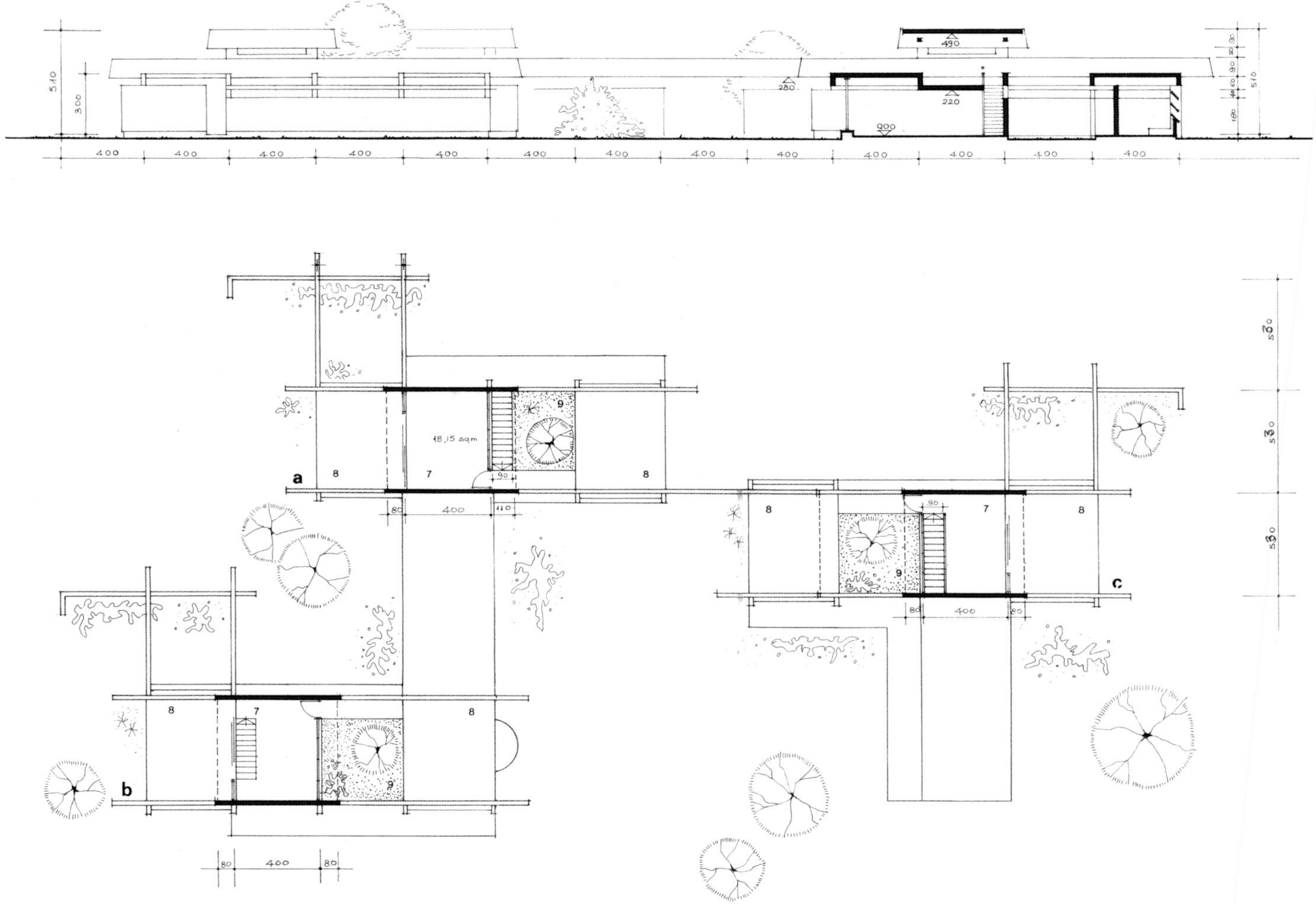

dwelling in auroville

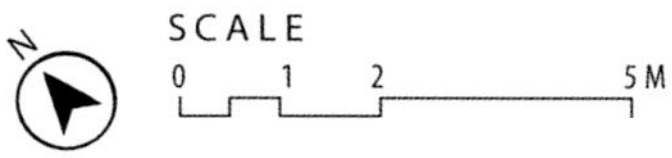

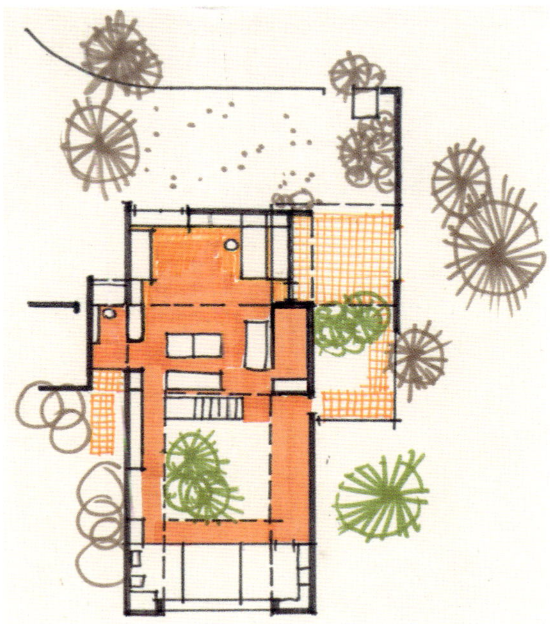

LEFT Interior courtyard with a simple wooden staircase to the loft, 1975

RIGHT ABOVE Entrance to the house of Piero and Gloria, a single door in a wall, 2012

RIGHT BELOW Sketch plan of the house highlighting the built versus open spaces

FACING PAGE First floor plan and conceptual section: A grid, comprising units of 4 x 5.3 m, overlays the site. Dimensions for the RCC structure and internal spaces are obtained from this. Each L-shaped unit comprises a single storey, a courtyard, a double storey, and a verandah, similar to the units employed in Auroson's Home.

The key concept in this cluster was to create pathways, gardens and solid exteriors that would provide privacy while protecting from the harsh sun of the tropical climate and the dust storms on the barren plateau of Auroville. The RCC frame structure has brick infill walls arranged in parallel at distances of 5.3 m. Long concrete beams separated from the walls highlighted a sense of horizontality and created strip windows to bring in light. These are ideal for hot-air ventilation, although at the time when these houses were built, the openings had fixed glass to keep out the dust and animals. The structure was originally entirely painted in white to create the sense of a singular white mass emerging from the surrounding sparse vegetation and to reduce the thermal radiation. The details of

ABOVE LEFT House of Piero and Gloria: Living-cum-work space, 1975

ABOVE RIGHT House of Piero and Gloria: Interior courtyard, 1975

BELOW In recent years, the courtyards have been covered by translucent polycarbonate roofing to keep away rain, mosquitoes, and thieves.

An outdoor verandah is attached to the living room. Extended beams create a sense of enclosure, framing the sky. A linear wall contains the verandah from one side, and is gently turned at the end to define the boundary. It directs the gaze towards the garden and to the Matrimandir scaffolding far on the horizon. Piero recalls an incident when once, after a particularly nasty dust storm, he could not see the scaffolding any more, and he rushed to the site on his cycle, only to find it still standing there to his relief! Photo: 1974

wooden sliding doors and fixed concrete louvres are similar to the ones used in Auroson's home in 1970. Entering the house through a single door within a long solid exterior wall lends a sense of subtlety and surprise. here is a complete world within as one enters the internal courtyard with a finely crafted wooden staircase on a stringer beam and large wooden sliding doors which enable openness between the courtyard and a living space with minimalistic setting having low cement platforms for sitting.

One of the three cluster houses was recently renovated for an elderly Aurovilian. "*As we are getting older, we need more comfort,*" says Gloria, explaining why they closed the courtyards with translucent roofing and added wire mesh on all the windows, with aluminium framing for sliding glass. "*In the earlier years, we didn't mind so much the mosquitoes, insects and rodents. But they were not as many as there are now!*"

ABOVE Living and reading space

LEFT Refurbished living room with inbuilt seating. Original wooden sliding doors are replaced with glass windows with wire mesh to bring in more light.
Photo: 2013, Jocelyn's House

The living space opens out into a court in the northwest. The use of wood in this particular project is noteworthy. Along with its use in pergolas at the entrance, wooden rafters form a mezzanine for the bedroom above this space, as seen in the photograph. The lines produced by these elements add visual richness and colour to the otherwise minimal interior space, adding rhythmic play between the horizontal and the vertical, between the light and shadow.

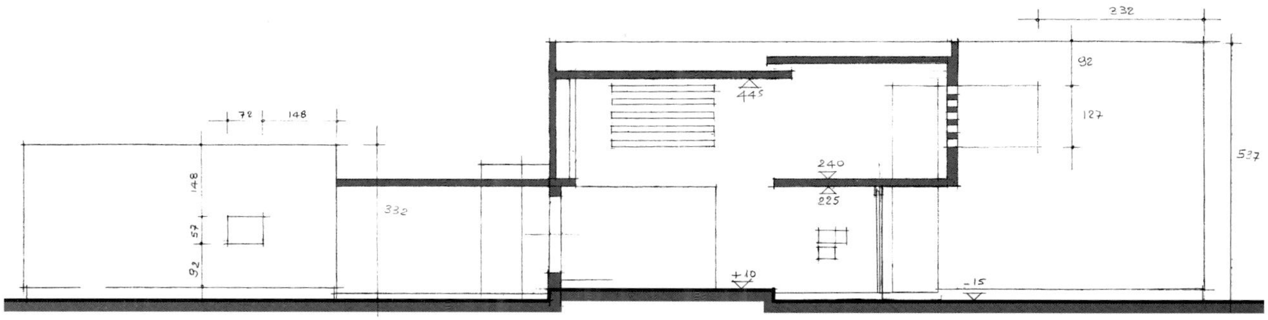

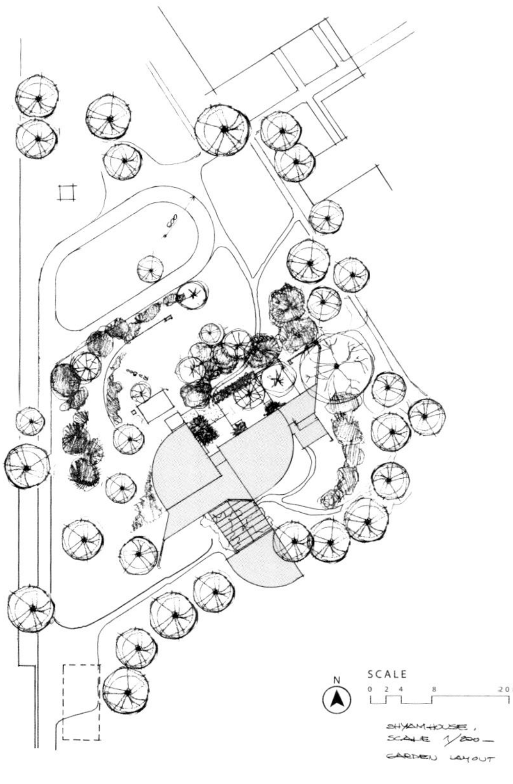

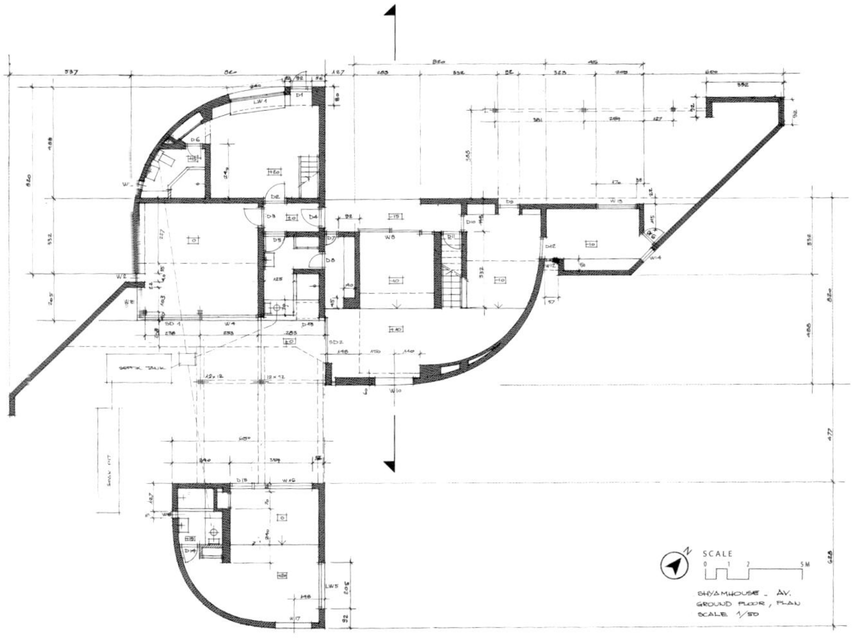

ABOVE, BELOW LEFT AND BELOW RIGHT
Section, site plan and ground floor plan. Solid and void spaces are placed in a dynamic configuration. The meeting of wall elements is accentuated by slits, and curved volumes lend an organic aesthetic.

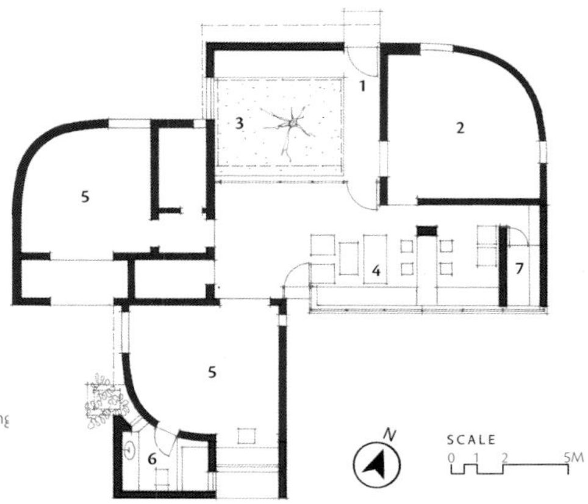

1. Entrance
2. Living
3. Courtyard
4. Kitchen/Dining
5. Bedroom
6. Bathroom
7. Storeroom

There was an initial attempt to design Shyamsunder's residence in line with the module concept in Andy's house (1975), where three square bedroom modules come together, each with one rounded corner. A large verandah serves as the interface between the three modules. However, Shyamsunder's house had very large area requirements too large to fit into a simple module concept. Eventually, the module became limited in use in the later works of Piero and Gloria.

A decade later, this unique combination of the softness of a quarter circle with the stability of a square edge was explored in another project: the Tagore Art Museum in Santiniketan. The four modules were combined here to form a large rounded enclosure, connected internally by perpendicular passages. Unfortunately, because of a change in the political setup in West Bengal, the project could not be realized.

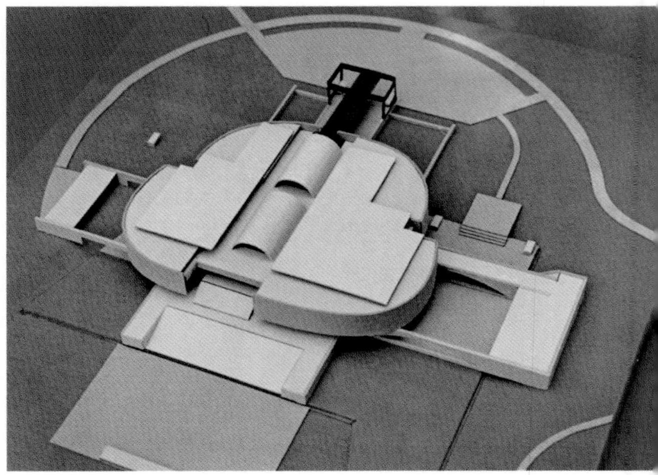

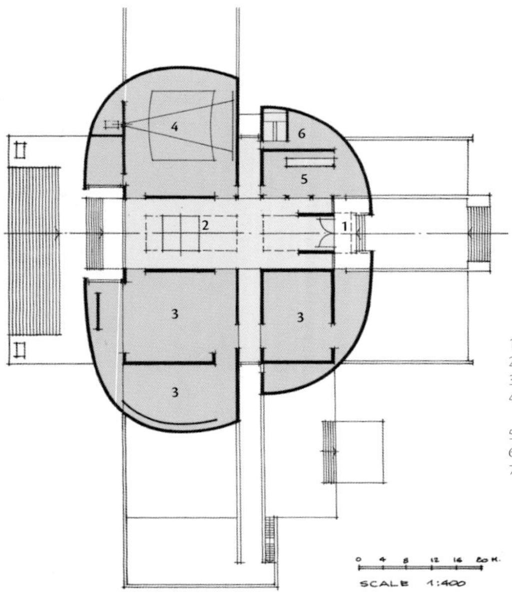

1. Entrance
2. Lobby
3. Museum
4. Auditorium and exhibtions
5. Counter
6. Utility
7. Open theatre

LEFT ABOVE
Andy's House, explorations of the same module in variations

RIGHT ABOVE
Plan and completed project, Andy's House, 1975

LEFT BELOW
Tagore Art Museum, explorations of the same module in variations

RIGHT BELOW
Plan and process model, Tagore Art Museum, Santiniketan, Calcutta, 1985 (unrealized)

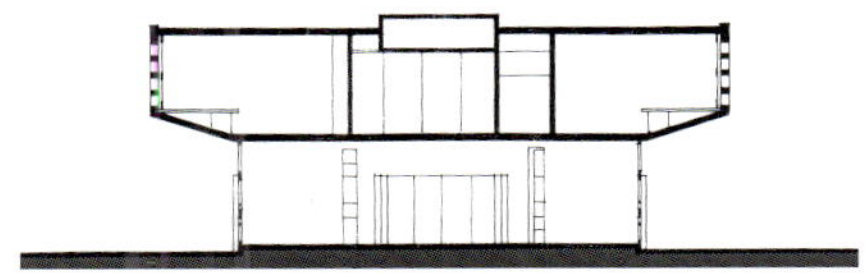

Roger Toll House

Auroville, 1973–1974

Another exploration of a replicable module is applied in Roger Toll House, which comprises three double-storey modules, each with a bedroom above and a common space below. Bedrooms are placed in the upper storey with beds placed on cantilever slabs, partially inspired by the section in Golconde Dormitories at the Sri Aurobindo Ashram, Pondicherry. Drawers for storage are placed below beds and were also built on site. The connecting slabs between the squarish bedrooms function as verandas, terraces, living room.

The house emerges from the ground ready to take flight, and the minor axis is oriented towards the Matrimandir. Perhaps proximity to the Matrimandir site, with no trees acting as barriers at the time of designing this building, dictated this. Angled and curvilinear walls counterbalance an urge to emerge with an urge to merge with the earth. Horizontal slits accentuate the sense of mass and diffuse the light in the interior spaces.

The Roger Toll house module was later repeated for a community house for nine people who wished to experiment by living together. The ground floor was to be used as common space. It was developed during 1976–79 as a collective called New Community, with rhythmic repetitions of the module.

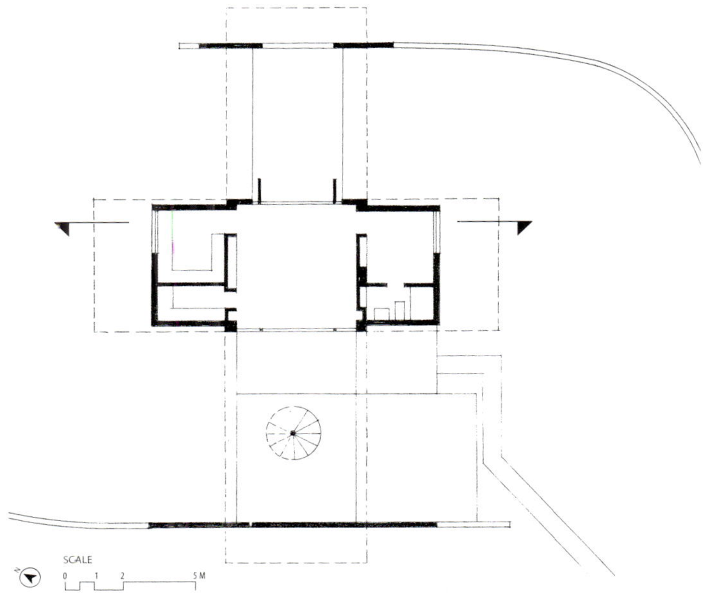

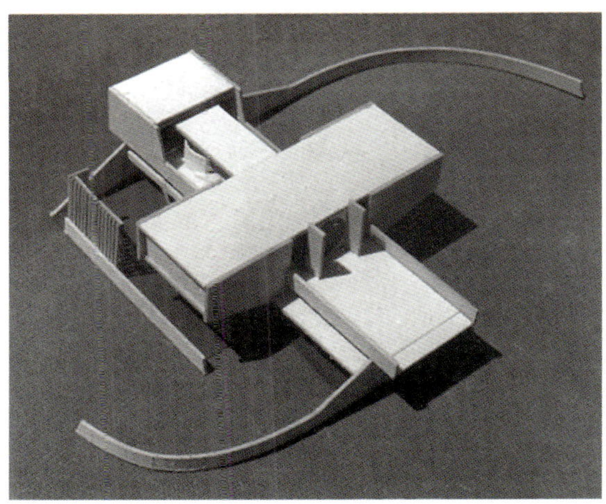

ABOVE AND CENTRE Section and plan of the Roger Toll house

BELOW A single module for the Roger Toll house

ABOVE Roger Toll House, 1974

BELOW LEFT AND RIGHT A steel spiral staircase with wooden treads, a masterpiece in workmanship, evoking the memory of Leonardo Ricci's Casa-studio project, Monterinaldi, Florence, 1952

ABOVE Large pivot doors enable openness between the verandah and living room.

BELOW Sketch of New Community cluster, 1977. A ramp appears as a central pivot in this dynamic volumetric ensemble.

Rika House

Certitude, Auroville, 1992–1993

In the few projects within Auroville that have been handled mainly by Gloria, one can appreciate her unique sensibility and sense of detailing. For Gloria, architecture is like music, poetry or the arts, and stems from a subtle creative intuition. In this particular project, her inspiration was the client herself: Rika, a *"fine lady with artistic qualities"*, the sort of ideal client that every architect would aspire to work with.

Believing that individual space is necessary "for the *sadhana*, for Auroville, for the yoga",[2] Piero and Gloria seek to create inward-looking spaces in the homes they design, which can lend a sense of containment set amidst nature.

Interestingly, Gloria decided to work with compressed cement stabilized earth blocks (CSEB) for this and a few other residences built in the early nineties. The Auram[3] mud block-making machine had then just been introduced in Auroville by French architect Satprem (Serge Maini), who hails from CRATerre research laboratory, Grenoble, and specializes in mud technology. Although rammed earth houses had been around for a long time in and around Auroville, especially in the village houses designed by Poppo Pingel, the Auram Press introduced a new phase of building with earth in Auroville. Its precise lines, fine visual quality, and the possibility to innovate on the size and shape of the blocks, perhaps prompted Gloria to explore this new material in their existing material and design palette. The choice also allowed one to be independent of the constantly changing prices of the bricks and the

North facade of Rika's House: The blank facade made of exposed mud blocks made on site is a deliberate attempt at responding to the busy road of the community in front, enhancing a sense of expectation and surprise for the approaching visitor.

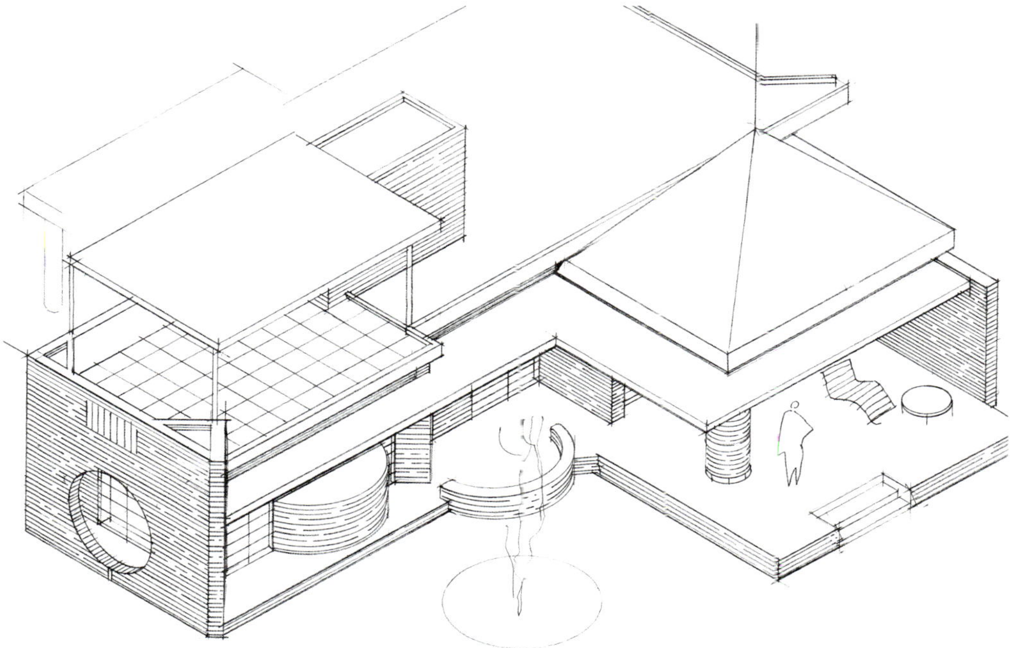

ABOVE LEFT Entrance towards the eastern porch: Rusticated brick columns and splayed edges of walls lend a tactile quality. The colours red, brown and white come together in a harmonious ensemble, stratifying the ascendance from ground upwards.

ABOVE RIGHT The play of volumes, circular wall and square windows at 45 degrees are typical elements in the vocabulary of Piero and Gloria.

BELOW Isometric sketch of Rika's house

As one enters the living room, across a spacious porch, one is instantly drawn towards a concave wall at the other end. This forms the heart of the space, with sky light and vistas into the garden in the east. There is a separation between planes as corners are accentuated to bring in light. A filler slab comprising T-beams and terracotta tiles adds alternating dark and light lines to the ceiling, which completes the visual composition of this space.

mafia around it. The blocks lend a sense of warmth that, coupled with the scales and careful attention to detailing in this house, lends an artistic and intimate character to the building.

Gloria's desire to experiment with these bricks was matched by Rika's enthusiasm for it. Rika's son, Andy, who had already been the contractor for the Phase II of the Health Centre and was working on the construction of the Matrimandir, became de facto contractor, making for a highly satisfactory collaboration.

The primary access of the Certitude community is east–west. Rika's house abuts this road on the south, with its northern face closed off from the busy road for privacy. The sense of entry is an indirect one, across the front yard and through a porch on the east that is masked by this wall.

"We think the design of details give richness and friendliness to a building. Difficult to define where begins the ornamentation," says Gloria. The living room and study room display Gloria's sensitivity towards each individual space and its detailing. This

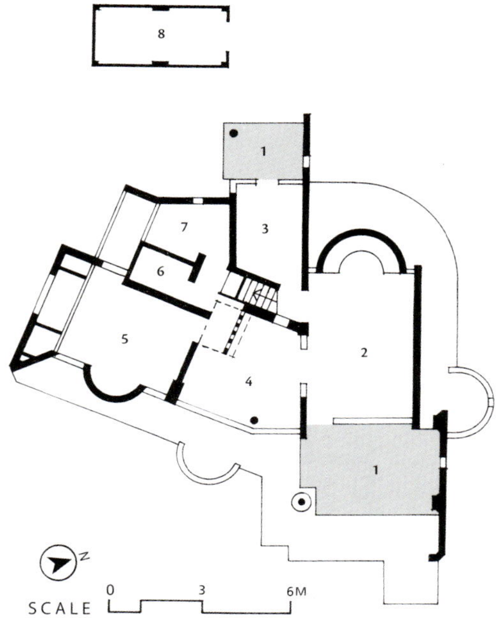

1. Verandah
2. Dining/Living
3. Kitchen
4. Studio
5. Bedroom
6. Store
7. Bathroom
8. Garage

care is applied in every space in the house, even in the bathroom, where a platform filled with pebbles borders a high square tub, lending a Zen quality to this space of bathing; or outside, where a lone stone lantern sits amidst a minimalist garden. A vertical mass anchoring the horizontal volumes acts as a wind funnel between the bedroom, bathroom and garden, circulating air.

Inspired in her younger days by the teachings of Leonardo Ricci, she says, "*Architecture is the space that is born from the gesture; it is linked to the existence. It is not something that comes from a dogma or the mind, or a principle. It is related to your life, not to a particular style. Harmony and beauty are the two things I myself need around me. These are the qualities I try to achieve in my work.*"[4]

"Nowadays one is bound to be existential, so to speak (not existentialist). Only those acts and consequently those forms which spring from man's existential truths and not from futile motives of taste will be fundamental... In a house one sleeps, eats and lives... Its value lies in the 'way' these acts are carried out."

—Leonardo Ricci, 1957[5]

LEFT The curve of the concave wall that forms the seating space in the living room is juxtaposed with the counter-plane of an arched beam that frames a visual continuum between the living-room spaces.

RIGHT Plan of Rika's house

Luise House

Verite, Auroville, 2004-2006

Piero and Gloria were asked to design this house for an Austrian aristocratic lady, Luise, who came to settle down in Auroville when she was almost 90, after having lived many years in Japan!

The place she chose was located in the Verite community, which occupies 8 acres in the industrial zone of Auroville. She had already built a house in this community some years before when she came as a long-term guest, but with age, she felt the need for more comfort. Most importantly, she wanted to bring her 50-year-old parrot to India from Japan. This trusted companion needed a well-designed home just as she did! The design brief included a living-cum-dining/kitchen space, a largish bedroom with attached bathroom and a small independent unit with a bedroom and a bathroom connected to her house for a caretaker.

Model explorations of the house show meticulous attention to the total composition, in terms of proportions and placement of the structural and non-structural elements such as free-standing columns. Several models are made in quick succession to study the same and the final design emerges after discussions with the client.

The building sits squarely on a high plinth with a new element in their vocabulary, a water channel acting as a deterrent to ants and other crawlies entering the

An extended RCC portal frame demarcates the entrance to the house creating an inviting entrance gesture towards a verandah space.

A large sliding door in metal with cloth-infill shutters separates the living and sleeping spaces. Here, once again, we see Piero's and Gloria's mastery of proportions and detailing. The detail was designed as a "*far echo of Japanese paper doors*," adds Piero, as Luise had lived for many years in Japan.

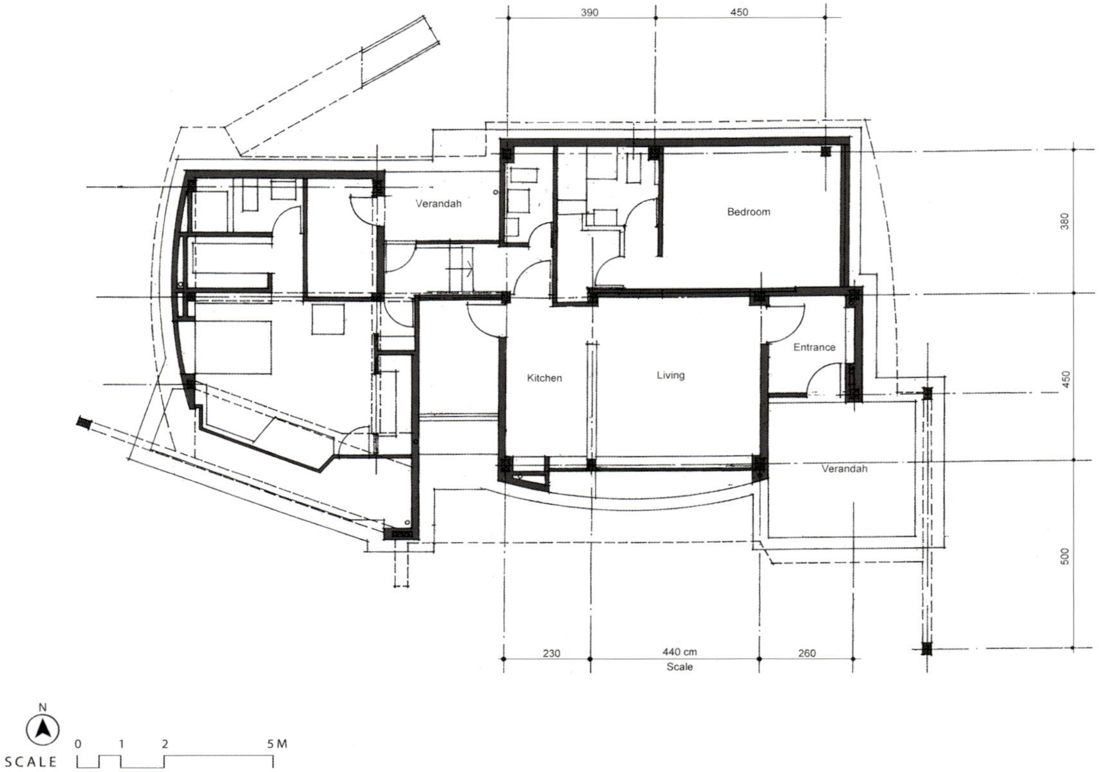

ABOVE Ground floor plan

BELOW A study model exploring proportions, overhangs, and structural and non-structural elements

FACING PAGE An extended RCC portal frame elongates the horizontality of the house's elevation and a secondary beam helps to break the sunlight streaming in.

house. The most prominent and striking element of this house is the entrance, which is pronounced by an RCC portal frame. It invites one to enter the verandah: a well-used space. The interior is well-lit, with easy-to-maintain ceramic tile flooring and skylight from a slit in the roof. The room for the parrot has forest-like paintings on the wall and a cage-like extension into the garden, a simple yet thoughtful gesture.

Unfortunately Luise lived only for a year in this house. Ever-changing occupants in buildings designed for special needs remains a challenge in Auroville, since there is no concept of personal property, keeping in mind the first point of the Auroville Charter:[6] "Auroville belongs to no one in particular, but to humanity as a whole...." New occupants invariably have different needs and changes are bound to happen, often not in harmony with the original design and intention of the architect. Currently, the building is used by the Verite community for hosting long-term researchers and guests to Auroville.

Notes

1. B.V. Doshi in a conversation in Auroville, March 2015.
2. *Auroville Today*, April 2012.
3. The Auroville Earth Institute came up with the original Auram Press, an in-house production in Auroville for compressed stabilized earth blocks.
4. *Auroville Today*, no. 205 (February 2006).
5. Published in December 1957. Domus published "a scheme for 15 houses" on the Monterinaldi hill overlooking Florence, where the architect Leonardo Ricci had transformed the steep slope of a stone quarry into an experiment in open housing.
6. See "The Context: Auroville—Unfolding of a Vision," p. 14.

Institutional Projects

Health Centre

Aspiration, Auroville 1972–1994

Phase I (1972–1976)

A health clinic that began in a temporary bamboo shelter started by Dr Sen in 1971, near the Aspiration huts, grew into a functional health centre around 1974. It catered to the needs of the small population of Aurovilians and the villagers from nearby, who often had no access to proper medical aid.

In those early years, each architectural project had to have a physical model presented to Roger Anger, the chief architect of Auroville, for approval. One can see the effect of this on many early buildings in Auroville, and the first phase of the Health Centre was no exception. A certain modularity and play of form, in keeping with Roger's Beaux Art tradition, was expected and this pushed Piero and Gloria to search for a vocabulary that was perhaps a challenge to their Italian–Finnish background. Piero points also to inspirations from the works of Finnish architect Reima Pietilä for these forms in the Health Centre.

As a result, the inclined granite walls of the first phase recall the kind of earth-hugging berms that Roger Anger had been exploring in the schools in Aspiration area during this time. The low, massive walls create a tension with the folded RCC slab that crisply "floats" above, as both wall and roof. The linear modules separate and unite intermittently to create courtyards and passages. Fixed concrete louvers, an oft-repeated element from their vocabulary, bring in diffused sunlight into the inner spaces. The ample overhang created by the inclined roof shades the louvered walls, heightening that illusory "floating" effect that is a hallmark of this couple's design sensibility.

FACING PAGE
Sketch of the Health Centre from southeast end

ABOVE LEFT Fixed concrete louvers bring in diffused sunlight into the inner spaces.

ABOVE RIGHT Perspective sketch by Piero of interior space between modules

BELOW Model of the entire (possible) modular extension

ABOVE Construction photo, 1974. The highest roof module ends with "floating" beams, accentuating a sense of lightness while bringing in light to the interior spaces.

BELOW LEFT Health Centre Phase I after completion

BELOW RIGHT School Building, Roger Anger, 1971

Phase II (1990–92)

Increase in population of both Auroville and the surrounding villages necessitated the expansion of the Health Centre. This addition now houses a waiting hall, patients' record counter, medical consultation rooms, pharmacy, laboratory for testing and administration offices.

Learning from Phase I, the extension was built to allow much more light and ventilation, making it a brighter space. The openness of the high-vaulted ceiling, with view on all sides towards nature, gives the effect of waiting within a garden. Curved lines in this new addition appear as a counterpoint to the strictly geometric lines of the existing folded RCC slab structure. Perhaps this was a subconscious choice to soften the space of the waiting hall, an attempt that Piero describes by saying, *"We tried, here, to avoid creating the clichéd, depressed and crowded waiting-room experience, to lessen the risk of contagion between 'unwell' individuals."*

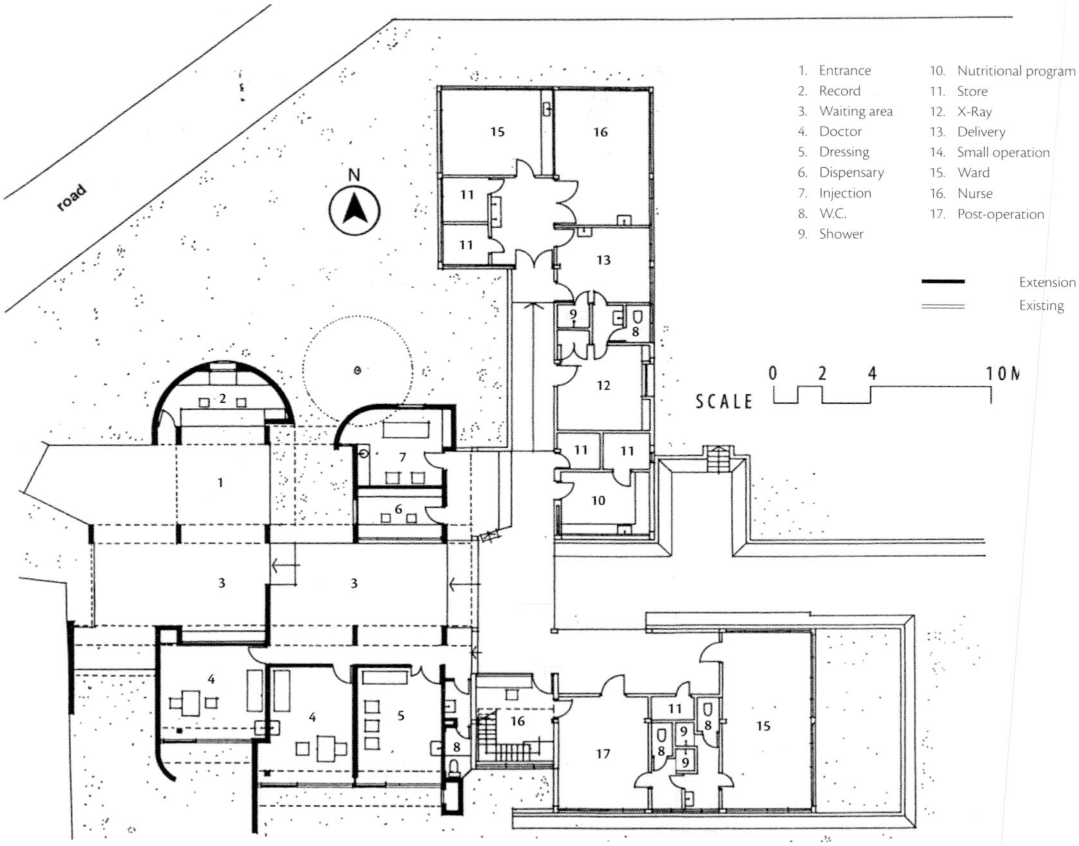

Plan of Phase II, Health Centre (1990–92) added to the existing building, 1972–76.

FACING PAGE

ABOVE LEFT View towards the ferrocement entrance vaults supported on piers

ABOVE RIGHT Section through catenary vault indicating shuttering detail

BELOW LEFT View towards courtyard where the vault stops to bring in light and nature in the patients' waiting hall.

BELOW RIGHT Gap between two curved walls at the waiting area reveals view towards court with water spout and fenestration details

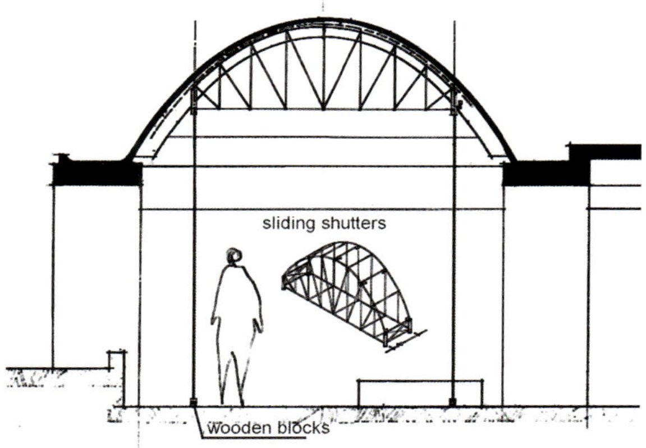
sliding shutters
wooden blocks

The curvilinear volumes soften the entrance vestibule of the Health Centre, and the use of textured finish on the piers that support the catenary vaults lends a tactile quality. Polished green cuddapah stone is used for cladding the wall and seating in the waiting area, making this space comforting to the eye and low on maintenance.

Although the extension to the existing structure employs rather different architectural features, the plan follows the overall linear north–south rhythm of the Phase I buildings. Two new ferrocement vaults though have their axes shifted perpendicular to the existing directionality, perhaps to create an "entrance" gesture more pronouncedly, and direct movement towards the Phase I building.

Additional Buildings (1998–2006)

1. Classroom
2. Toilets
3. Computer room
4. Office
5. Theatre workshop

Existing Buildings (1985–1998)

6. Library
7. Classrooms
8. Common hall
9. Body awareness hall
10. Dining room
11. Art and Craft
12. Staff quarters

Site plan of Transition School, 2005

Transition School

Auroville 1985–2005

Unending education and constant progress are mentioned in the second article of the Charter of Auroville[1] and, therefore, present themselves as a fundamental characteristic of life in Auroville. Schools in Auroville do not follow any specific predetermined course material but evolve their own methods as per the demands and capacities of the teachers and students alike. There is no certificate system, and the student–teacher ratio is low. All subjects are taught with special emphasis on language, art and sports. In short, the education offered in the various schools of Auroville values the uniqueness of each human being and seeks to help them realize their full creative power and potential within.

In 1984, the Indian government, through the Sri Aurobindo International Institute for Education and Research (SAIIER), began financing education projects for Auroville. Under this scheme, the first phase of the Transition Campus was initiated in 1985. Piero and Gloria explain: "*The projects have been done in close collaboration with the teachers, who are committed to the research and development of a new kind of education. It is necessary to give the Auroville children the possibility to receive a good education in Auroville and not be obliged to seek it elsewhere in India or abroad. The challenge was to find a teaching method and a design that would balance the freedom necessary for the growth of the soul and of creativity, with a structured organization that would lend the children security and stability without being oppressive.*"

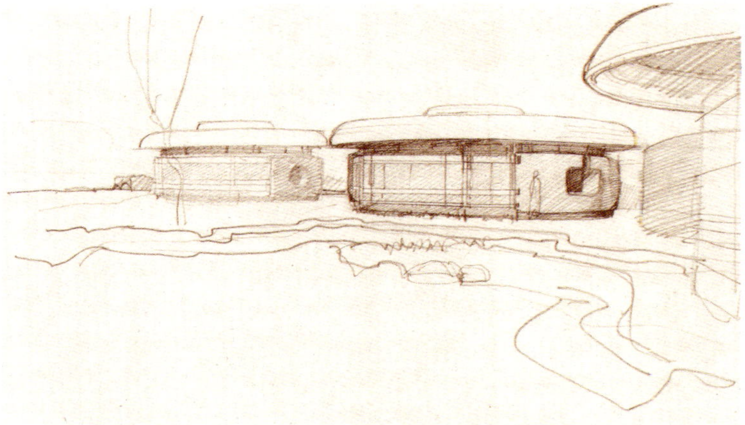

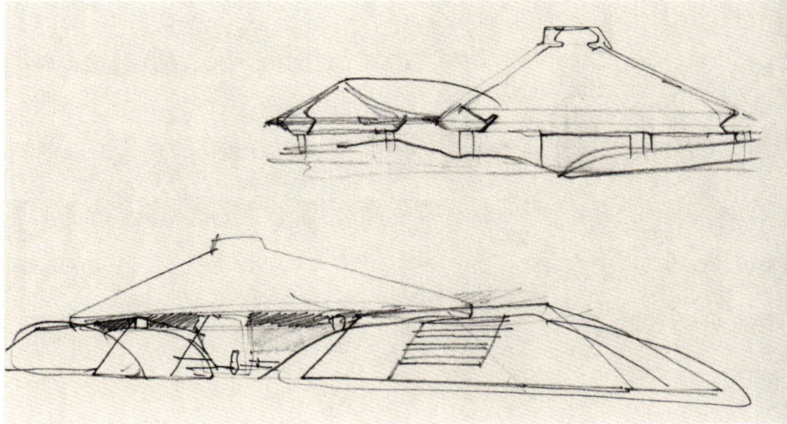

ABOVE LEFT AND RIGHT Exploratory sketches of classrooms by Piero

BELOW Children using a common area vaulted in ferrocement, adjacent to a classroom, 1986

LEFT A classroom with ferrocement roof: ribbon windows lend the illusion of separation between horizontal and vertical elements.

RIGHT Common area in between classrooms

This research is reflected in the various layouts and shapes of the buildings existing on the 9-acre campus. In Phase I, the classrooms were dispersed, intimate and round, in the manner of a more informal kind of teaching. In the following phases it became clear, with the increasing number of children, that a less scattered and more traditional kind of classroom was needed that could accommodate up to 20 students, whilst retaining connection with nature. Today, the Transition Campus provides a learning environment for 160 children between the ages of six and14.

Phase I (1985–86)

"Personally, we like to live as much as we can in nature," explains Piero. *"And we wish Auroville could maintain its buildings immersed in nature. We avoid cutting trees, even when they are very close to where we have to build. The challenge is to create an architecture that protects the human being from the extremes of the climate, the aggression of other human beings, and the disturbance of a certain kind of animal life, without depriving one of the beauty, the richness and the harmony of nature, and without depriving nature of its own space and life."*

This philosophy especially comes into play in the design of the Transition Campus. The design is a welcome solution to the present problem of modern schools being seen as "human factories",[2] whose prevalence is leading to more and more standardized spaces for rigid educational systems. Piero's and Gloria's designs strive to express the balance between body, mind and spirit that the school's pedagogy, based on ideas of integral development, seeks to instil. Classes often spill out into the open spaces, and poetry lessons are held under trees.

The school projects of Piero and Gloria reveal a certain restraint shown in avoiding the manicuring of the surrounding landscape. A belief in the untamed spirit of nature living in harmony with the manmade is perhaps a subconscious reason for the same. Children who spend their formative years in such a space, cannot but develop a holistic understanding of their role in the world with respect to the environment.

The music hall (1985) is designed for good acoustics, with possibility of spill-outs for musical and theatrical performances. The curves lend a cave-like sense of

ABOVE Transition School campus, 1985

BELOW LEFT Classroom clusters, Transition School Phase 1, 1985, plan and section through classroom and common area

BELOW RIGHT Ferrocement roof construction

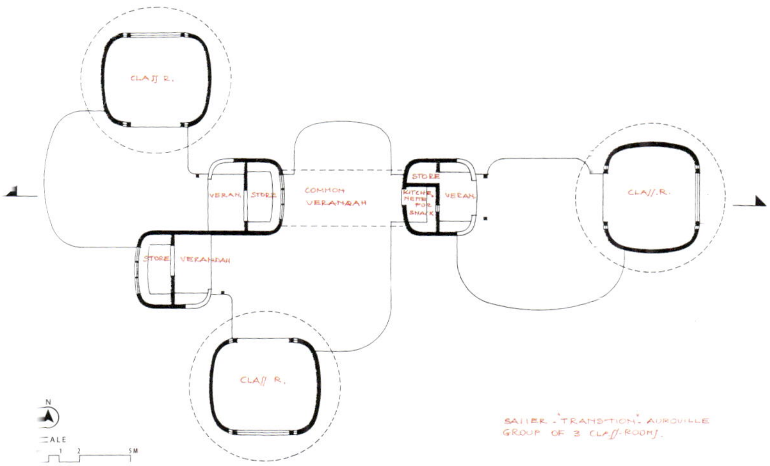

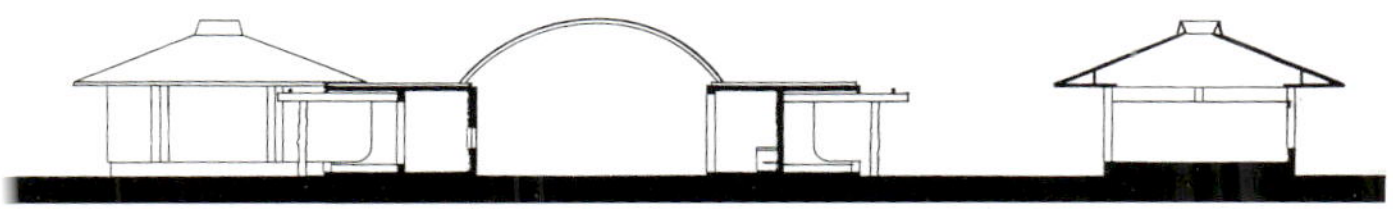

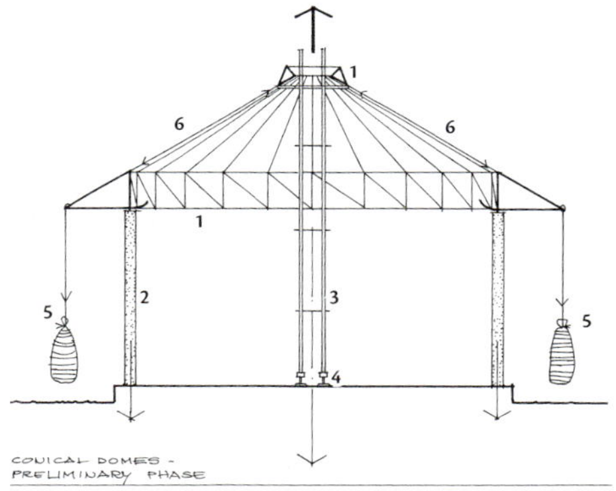

1. Ring beam (TS 12-mm dia., welded joints)
2. Columns
3. Props
4. Screw Jacks to lift top ring and give radial tension to MS 6-mm dia. rods
5. Removable sand bags used as balancing load
6. Radially pre-stressed MS 6-mm dia. rods to remain in ferrocement shell

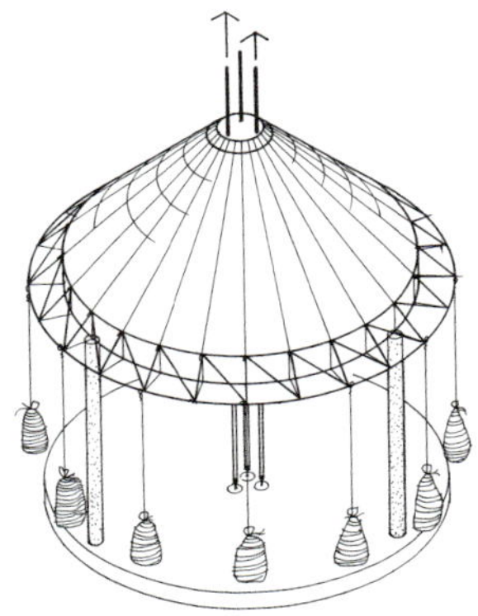

containment, and an oculus brings in light through the ferrocement roof.

Regarding their explorations of forms, Piero and Gloria explain, "*Sometimes we use angles of different degrees, asymmetric geometrical figures, and curves composed by segments of circles with different diameters. We believe they help soften the spaces or adapt the building to a better orientation. They lend the buildings and their outside spaces friendliness, especially in the schools, and create more harmony with the teaching methods of Auroville.*"

ABOVE AND BELOW
Music hall and amphitheatre, 1985

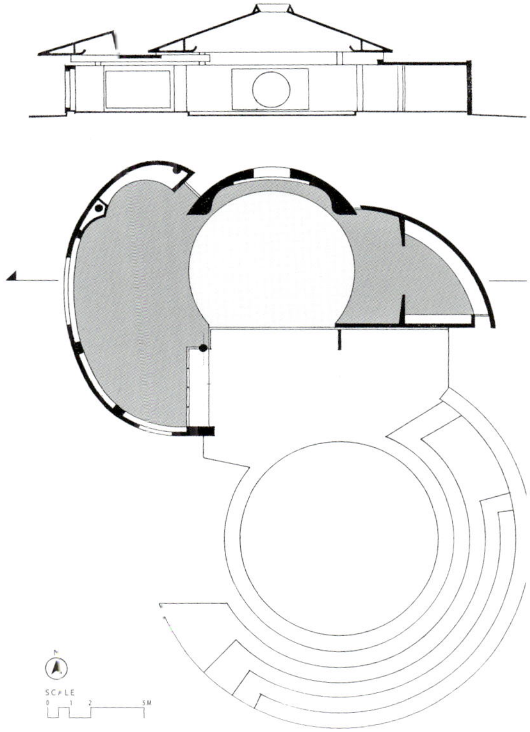

ABOVE LEFT Carefully detailed gaps for light in corners where two walls meet

ABOVE RIGHT Transition School music hall, section and plan

BELOW LEFT Music hall interior: Diffused light bathes the ceilings through ribbon windows

BELOW RIGHT Extended beam, resting on a free-standing column (not seen here), acts as a 'gateway' into the amphitheatre.

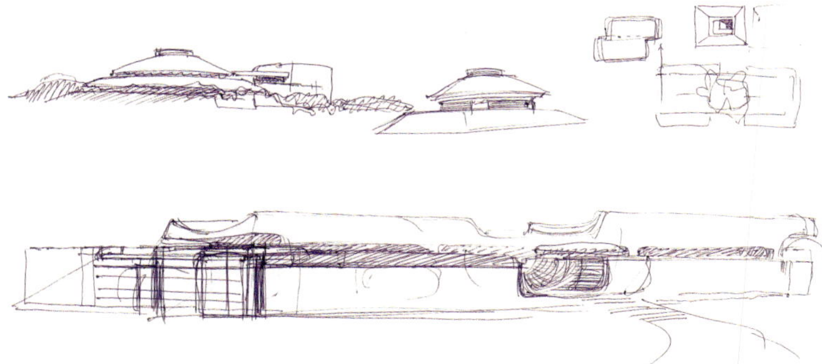

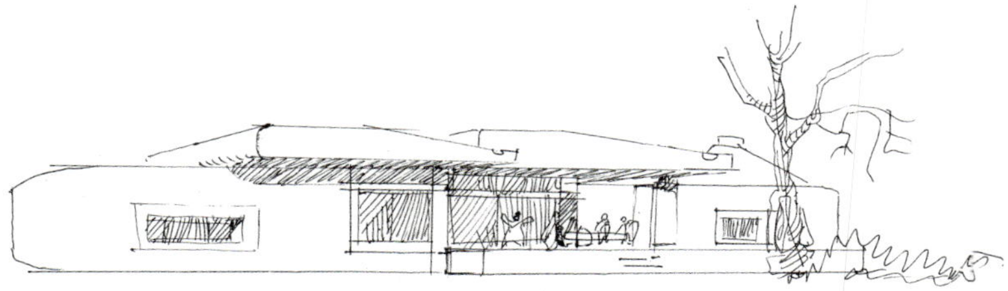

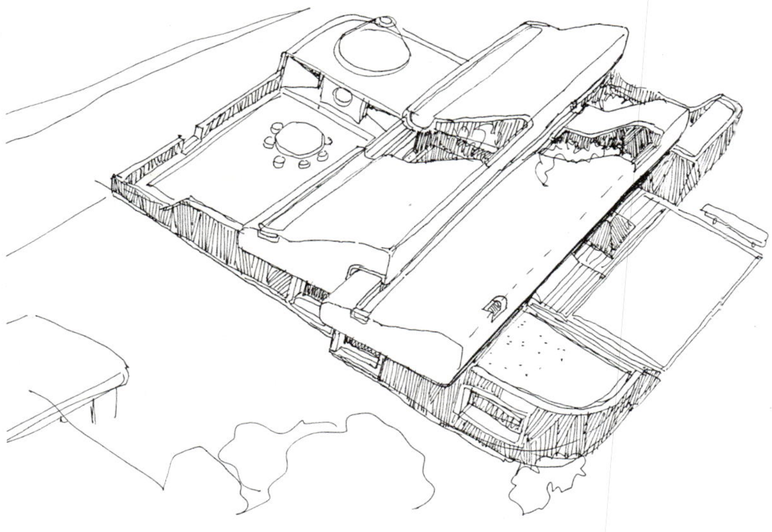

LEFT ABOVE
Angled walls and ferrocement roofs

LEFT BELOW 15 m-dia. gymnasium dome in ferrocement, resting on four points, built at Certitude sports ground, 1987

RIGHT ABOVE
Exploratory sketches

RIGHT CENTRE
Workshop sketch

RIGHT BELOW Workshop sketch, exploring asymmetrical roof form and curves

One of the characteristics of the Phase 1 at Transition School campus was the experimental use of ferrocement roofs. Most of these roofs, used over roundish plans, were having conical shapes This shape is structurally working as a very effective thin shell. Additionally the conical shape helps to pull a number of radial tendons to obtain and maintain a higher density in the cement and eventually prevent capillary cracks. These roofs are still well preserved after thirty years. Similar conditions can be seen the 15-m diameter gymnasium dome in the Certitude playground and the catenary vaults of the Health Centre, both of which were designed as thin shells at about the same time.

On the other hand, exploration of asymmetrical roof forms and curves with ferrocement shells in the design of Transition School workshops ended with unforeseen waterproofing problems. In order to continue using the buildings comfortably, the ferrocement roof was eventually totally wrapped in aluminium sheets.

Phase II (1994–99)

Mary, a teacher in Auroville for 30 years, aptly says, “Everyday, I discover something new on this campus while walking through it.” This is in keeping with the spirit of the “unending education” that Auroville aspires for.

The children take ample advantage of this sprawling campus, running around in their playtime and playing volleyball, climbing the two “safe” trees on campus, or simply seeking a moment of solitude in the Quiet Gardens behind the latest ATB (Awareness through the Body) Hall. The choice of low density

Courtyard around existing trees in the dining hall at Transition School

ABOVE Isometric view of Dining Hall, kitchen and ATB Hall

BELOW Dining Hall, Kitchen and ATB (Awareness Through the Body) Hall with landscaping

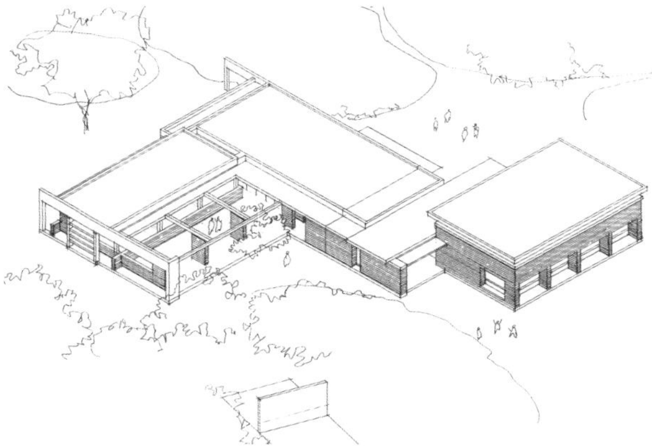

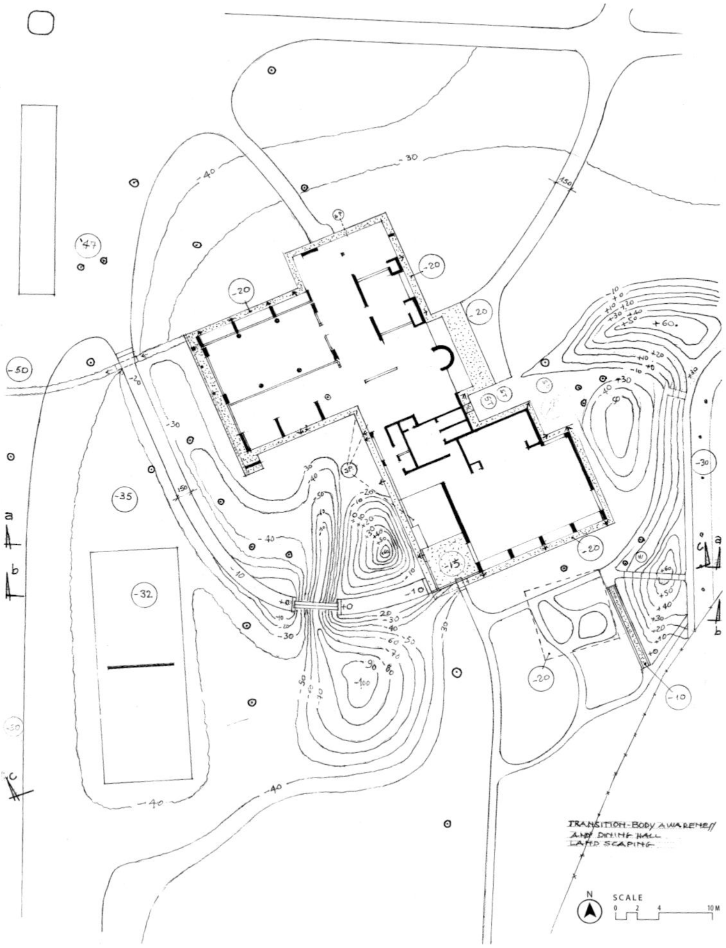

in campus planning is a practical one, based on the need for ample cross-ventilation that the warm-humid climate of coastal Tamil Nadu necessitates. It also facilitates the campus expansion in phases, as the money trickles in, and allows for diffusion of sound.

Over the different phases of the Transition School, one can see a gradual progression from freedom to structure. The teachers increasingly wanted to have more control as the number of students grew. The money, which often came through Government of India grants, needed more bureaucratic paperwork and there was less possibility to experiment. In spite of this, Piero and Gloria managed to create a sense of continuity between scales and materiality that defines the Transition Campus.

The classrooms have large openings with deep overhangs, creating internal environments that are airy. The rooms wrap around the edges of trees, generating courtyards that bring more light into the internal spaces. A local sedimentary stone, cuddapah, is used for flooring, which soothes the bare feet of the children, as the culture of removing footwear while entering a place of learning remains an essential one in Auroville.

As Louis Kahn, the great American architect, says: "... Schools began with a man under a tree, who did not know he was a teacher, discussing his realization with a few, who did not know they were students... You get an order from the school board that says, 'We have a great idea. We should not put windows in the school, because the children need wall space for their paintings, and also windows can distract from the teacher.' Now, what teacher deserves that much attention? I'd like to know. Because after all, the bird

ABOVE, CENTRE LEFT & RIGHT Dining Hall, Transition School, 1996. As in most of Piero's and Gloria's buildings, accentuated horizontality remains a key characteristic feature, giving a sense of serenity and scale. The plastered walls are painted the 'Auroville red' colour to integrate them into the landscape.

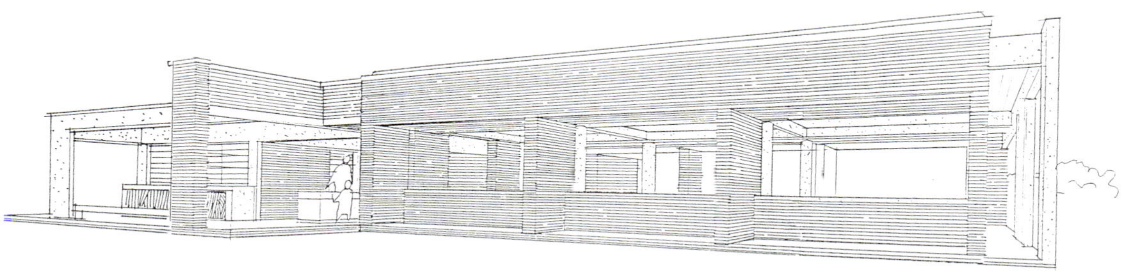

BELOW Perspective sketch of the dining hall. Extended beams on free-standing walls characterize transitions between spaces, like 'gateways', lending scale and extending the built form into the garden.

outside, the person scurrying for shelter in the rain, the leaves falling from the tree, the clouds passing by, the sun penetrating: these are all great things. They are lessons in themselves. Windows are essential to the school, you are made from light, and therefore you must live with the sense that light is important. Such a direction for the school board telling you what life is all about must be resisted. Without light, there is no architecture."[3]

Phase III (1999–2009)

Two important additions were built during this period of time. The first was a classroom with space for more than 20 computers, along with a large classroom and an administrative office. The second addition included four classrooms and toilets.

As part of their requirements, the teachers insisted on having pronounced overhangs for the classrooms in order to protect the walls from rain and sun. The language of the Phase II buildings is, therefore, marked by accentuated overhangs that appear to "float" above the walls, an effect heightened by recessed ribbon windows.[4]

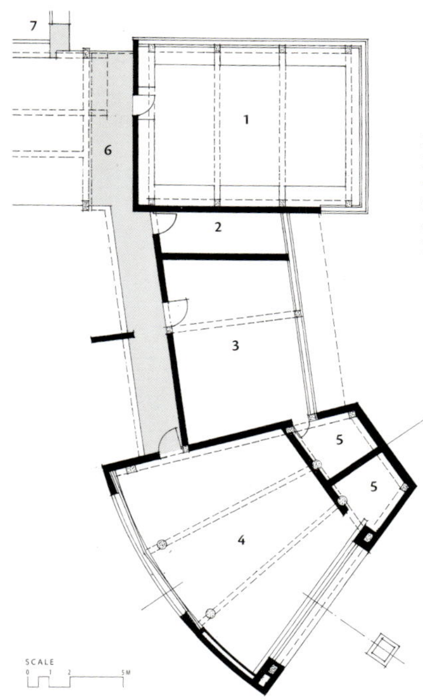

ABOVE Additional computer classroom and administration building

BELOW Drawings of Transition School classrooms

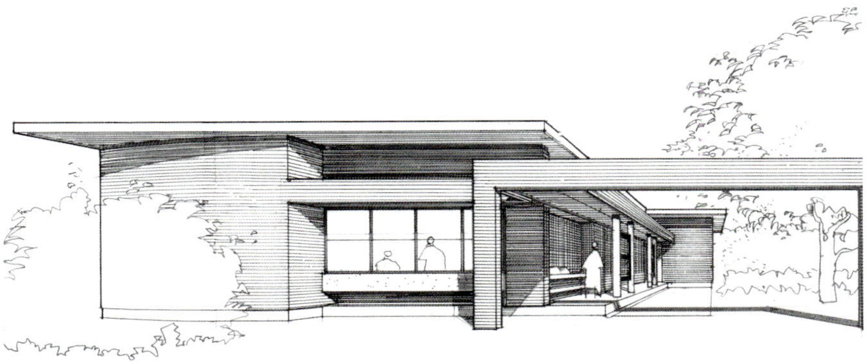

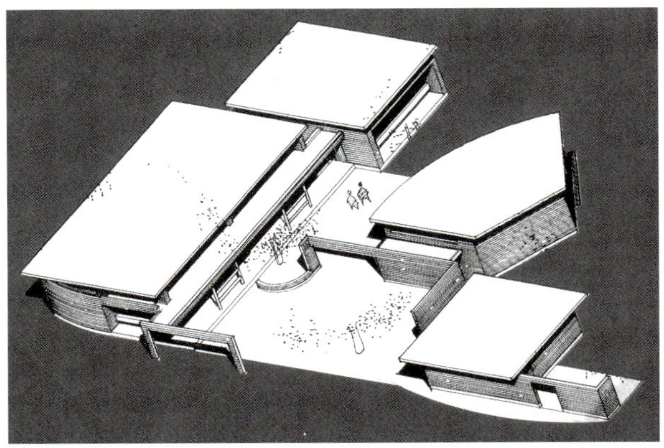

Four additional classrooms
and toilet block

Future School

Auroville 2000–2003

A high school for 90 students, Future School was constructed with the blessing of a big donation made by a computer company in Auroville. It displays a fine tuning in the language that Piero and Gloria had started to develop during Phase II of Transition School. Around the year 2000, there was no high school in Auroville (after Transition School, primary level) with a scientific direction and corresponding laboratories. Many children were obliged to go to schools outside Auroville or in Western countries. So, a young teacher, Chali, proposed a complete programme for such a facility in Auroville and approached Piero and Gloria for the project. They designed it in close and harmonious collaboration with her and the future teachers.

"Only during the construction of Transition and Future School did we start to enjoy the help of a contractor," says Piero. *"What a surprise! Times were changing! Less time was wasted in running around to search and buy materials, or to be on site for the execution. More time could be spent with the project, with drawings and study models! Younger architects in Auroville today don't realize how fortunate they are!"*

A self-made contractor, German-born Rolf Redis, in spite of building in a context that was far removed from his country of origin, was not only an organized and efficient professional with his unit Sumark, but was also a close collaborator and instrumental in introducing Piero and Gloria to his special construction assembly for roofing: a variation of the famous "Madras roof"[5] without timber.

LEFT Aerial view showing three defined centres enveloped by the buildings

RIGHT View towards courtyard from the transition space

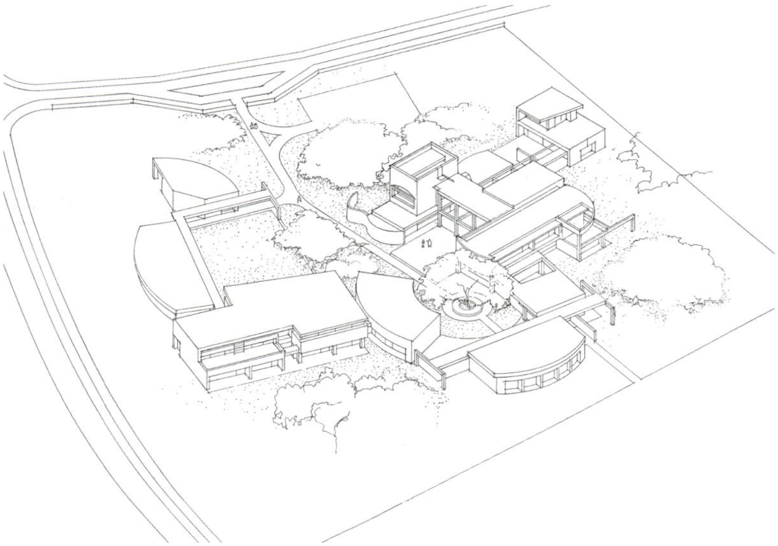

Curves and rectilinear geometries respond to each other gently, coming together in a harmonious ensemble that lends a sense of containment, balanced with openness.

Proposed plan: layout at ground level

1. Entrance
2. Parking area
3. Plaza
4. Library
5. Computer classroom
6. Classroom
7. Teachers
8. Toilets
9. Assembly hall/Theatre
10. Backstage
11. Silent room
12. Arts and crafts hall
13. Wood/Metal workshop
14. Dining room
15. Recreation
16. First aid/Medical Facility
17. SAIIER office/ Administration

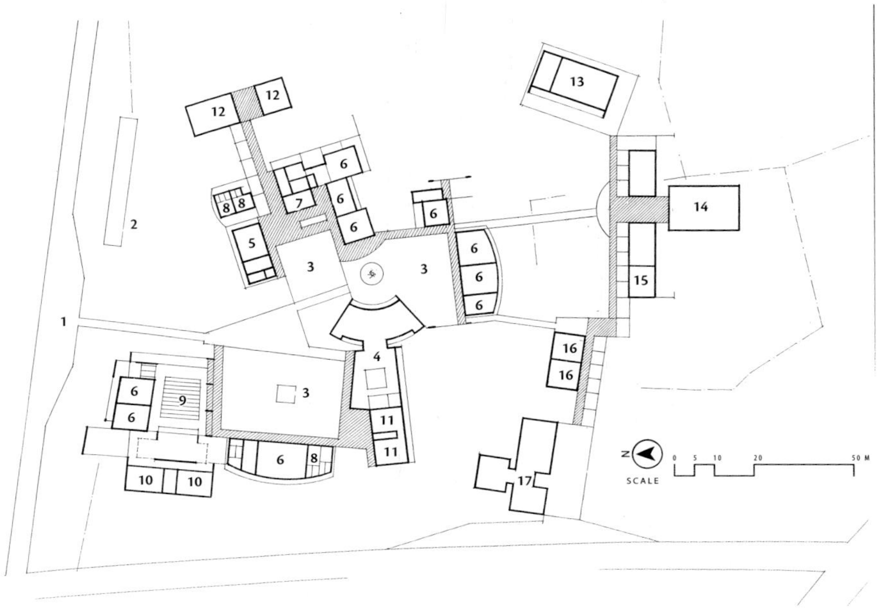

Proposed plan: layout at level 1

4. Library
6. Classroom
9. Auditorium/Theatre
19. Presentation room
20. Biology
21. Physics
22. Chemistry

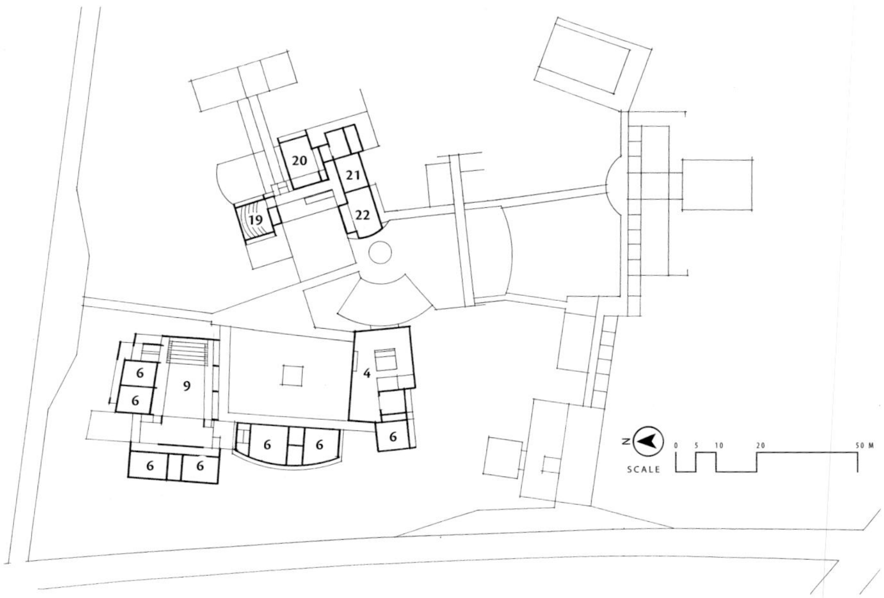

Original layout of overall campus of Future School—ground floor and first floor plans. Here, one sees a clear intention to create a campus that revolves around open spaces and yet allows for an interesting interplay of volumes and axes. However, over the years, many parts have been changed or not been realized.

ABOVE Model of Future School

BELOW Free curved walls lend dynamism to the U-shaped plan, almost indicating a torque that is anchored by the free-standing staircase in the central foyer.

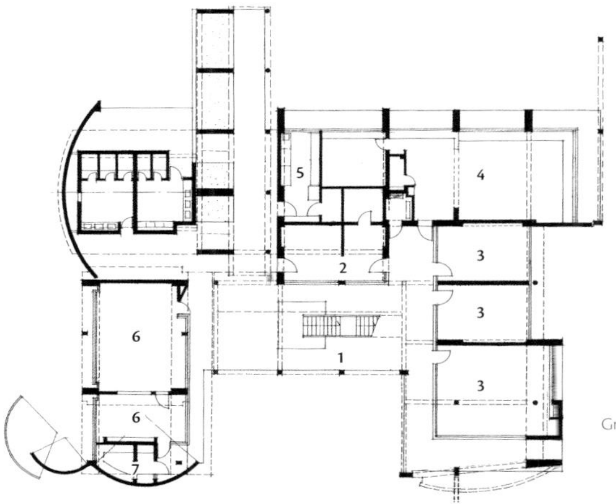

Ground Floor Plan

1. Entrance
2. Staff room
3. Classroom
4. Library
5. Kitchen
6. Computer room
7. UPS room

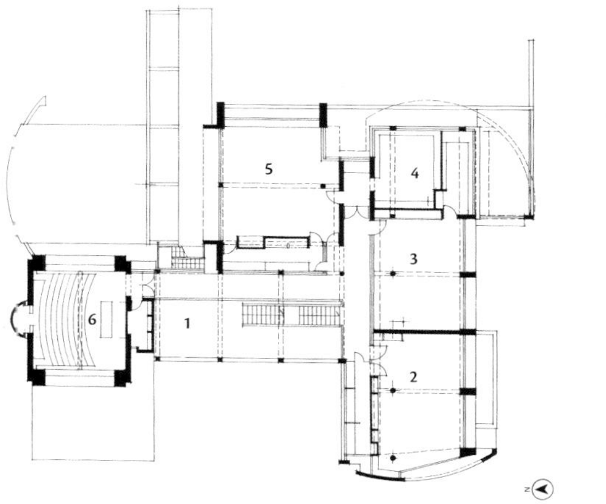

First Floor Plan

1. Verandah
2. Chemistry lab
3. Physics lab
4. Science store
5. Biology lab
6. Presentation

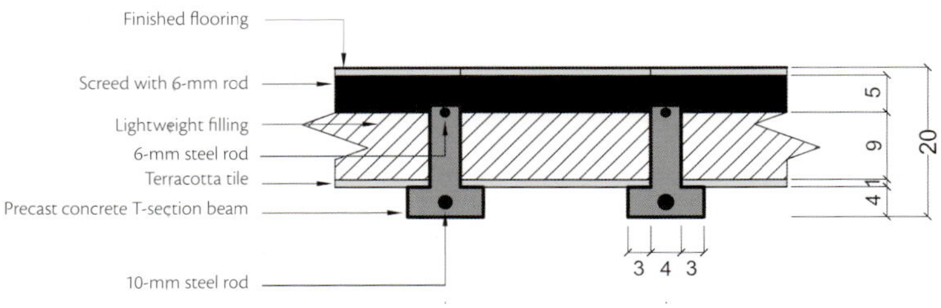
Finished flooring
Screed with 6-mm rod
Lightweight filling
6-mm steel rod
Terracotta tile
Precast concrete T-section beam
10-mm steel rod
5
9
4
1
4
20
3 4 3

ABOVE Two vertical elements anchor the seamlessly flowing landscaped space—a vertical volume for the presentation room and a tall rock in the garden.

BELOW Students on the first floor of the classroom block. The image shows the under-surface of the adapted "Madras roof" ceiling.

FACING PAGE The flat slab roof construction is a variation of the traditional "Madras roof" technique, using reinforced precast concrete inverted "T"-beams that span across at intervals of 39 cm. Hollow terracotta blocks are placed between the T-beams, which provide heat insulation as well as structural filling. This method of construction spares the need to use shuttering, while creating an under-surface for the ceilings that is warm in appearance.

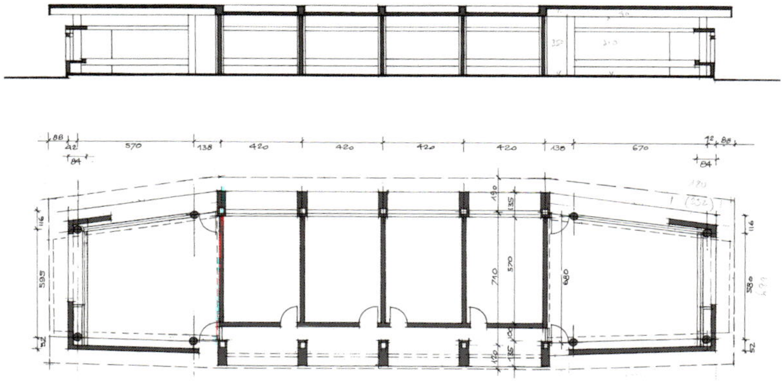

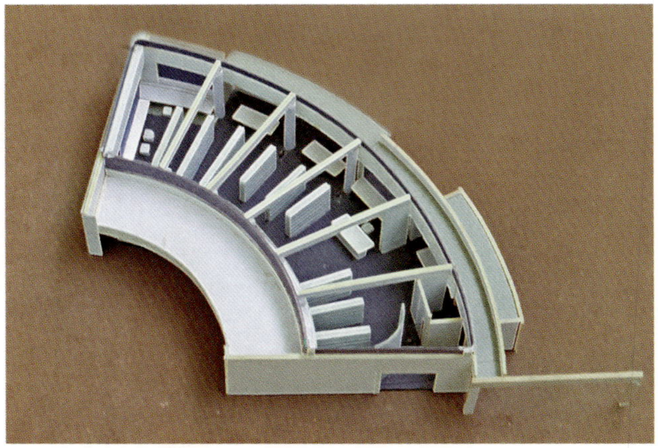

ABOVE LEFT Learning laboratories, Future School campus, ground floor plan

ABOVE RIGHT Model of Library

BELOW LEFT Learning laboratories: Recesses between vertical and horizontal elements accentuate a sense of separation, and the masses seem to rest lightly. The elements are arranged in a clear and rhythmic composition.

BELOW RIGHT Library with low-height reading space and double-height shelf space. Ample natural light floods this generous volume from above.

LEFT ABOVE A sense of horizontality and mass is balanced by the floating impression of lightness. Free beams are suspended from the slab by steel supports to moderate the abrupt transition from light to heavy, giving a sense of scale and breaking the sunlight streaming in.

LEFT BELOW AND RIGHT Pebbles mark thresholds between the built and unbuilt. There is a play of form and fluidity and an evident tension as a circular mass rests on a square plan, lending interest and creating deep overhangs.

UNITY PAVILION

International Zone, Auroville, 2001–2013

The idea for Unity Pavilion was conceived in the mid-nineties. Architect B.V. Doshi, who has been part of the governing board of Auroville (2010–16), had emphasized on the importance of the International Zone in anchoring the various cultures of the world. The Unity Pavilion was envisaged as a building that would be "an expression of inclusiveness",[6] a platform allowing also for the smaller countries to contribute to Auroville, marking a crucial foundation for the manifestation of the International Zone in Auroville.

The Unity Pavilion is located on one of the main future arteries of Auroville, the Crown Road, that should unite all the four zones in a circular movement around the Matrimandir. Several other institutional buildings such as Bharat Nivas, Savitri Bhavan, Tamil Heritage Centre and the Language Lab are located in this area. In future, this zone will be the public face of Auroville with all nations having their cultural pavilions.

The programme necessitated the creation of a place that would facilitate interactions based on harmony and collaboration, and comprises currently of a multipurpose hall, an office, a "Hall of Peace" and a caretaker's house. As in every other project, Piero takes care of the structural engineering as well, allowing him a greater freedom to incorporate the structure into the building design from the very beginning.

Piero proposed the Hall of Peace as a special section of the Unity Pavilion, to house the Peace Table for Asia,[7] which was crafted by master wood-craftsman George Nakashima and was donated to Auroville by

View towards the entrance foyer, pivoted around a vertical tower. The structure is RCC with brick infill. Akin to several of their projects, punctures and slits in the walls of the surrounding forms accentuate a sense of mass, creating an opposition to the sense of openness that characterizes the Unity Pavilion's ground floor halls.

ABOVE Play of of mass and volume on north facade

BELOW A horizontally extending beam accentuates the primary entry axis

FACING PAGE, ABOVE
View towards the office entrance in the south. The thick brick walls are non-structural and lend a sense of perceptual ambiguity with a thick slab seemingly floating above. The walls conceal behind them the structural columns, lending solidity to the facade. Horizontal grooves in the plastering provide a sense of scale and pebbles mark the threshold between the built and unbuilt, like in the school projects.

BELOW View towards a multipurpose hall that faces southwest. Additional beams are suspended characteristically by circular steel sections from the structural beams to lend scale and provide additional shade. Grills provide security on the exterior transparent faces, and frameless glass doors in the interior enable openness for the southwest breeze when large gatherings take place in the hall.

ABOVE AND BELOW

Multipurpose hall at Unity pavilion, 2012. The Peace Table was temporarily placed here, awaiting the completion of the Hall of Peace.

FACING PAGE

ABOVE

Interior view of the Hall of Peace

BELOW

Inside the Hall of Peace during a congregation, 2014

Notes

1. See 'The Context: Auroville—Unfolding of a Vision', p. 14
2. Hugo Kuekelhaus, *Inhuman Architecture* (Auroville: Studio Naqshbandi, 2007).
3. John Lobell, *Between Silence and Light. Spirit in the Architecture of Louis L. Kahn*, 47.
4. Ribbon windows: In the 1920s, architect Le Corbusier developed what would later be known as "The Five Points of Modern Architecture": 1) Supports, or pilot is; 2) Roof gardens; 3) Free design of ground plan; 4) Horizontal, or ribbon window, and 5) Free design of the facade.

   These interrelated design considerations were responses to industrialization, the use of reinforced concrete, and making a break with traditional buildings. They are most evident in the architect's famous "Villa Savoye" outside Paris. They became emblematic of a new direction in architecture, besides being a polemical statement for modern architecture.
5. Madras roofing, Transition school: This is a traditional flooring/roofing technique, particularly practiced in south India. It involves the use of wood and "*aachikal*" (a local small brick) and lime plaster. Commonly used for small spans. Wooden beams are used to cover the span of less than 45cm from each other. The gaps between is filled with "*aachikal* bricks" laid on edge in a diagonal fashion with lime plaster.
6. Quote Jaya, "The main hall of the Unity Pavilion opens," *Auroville Today* (April 2012): 6.
7. Peace table: Some twenty-five years ago, Master wood-craftsman George Nakashima conceived the idea of offering to each continent of the world a Table for Peace, crafted from two great 300-year-old Eastern Black Walnut. The Peace Table for Asia was inaugurated in Auroville on 29 February 1996.
8. *Auroville Today*, no. 205 (February 2006).

What Architecture Cannot Be

Poppo Pingel

And twofold Always.
May God us keep
From Single vision
And Newton's sleep!
—William Blake[1]

On 28 February 1968, I had the privilege of putting the German soil into the urn at the inaugural ceremony of the Auroville project. Six months later in August 1968, fortunately, my German organization granted me a study trip to Pondicherry. The euphoria of joining Auroville was still very intense, and there was a growing urge to know more about it.

In those days, Auroville's focal point was the impressive unearthly view from the sky of Roger Anger's "galaxy model" (for the city), which attracted many including me. After having worked and lived in a village, 20 km away from the next tar road, in famine stricken Bihar in 1967, my overwhelming question was, how are they going to deal with the 20,000 local Tamilians in the villages surrounding and within the city master plan? The answers I received from the architects and managers were unsatisfactory to me. It seemed to me as if they had completely overlooked this obviously challenging fact.

Things changed on meeting Gloria and Piero in August 1968 at Promesse, the first settlement of Auroville. They were the first architects already living on Auroville soil. Indeed, talking to them was an eye-opener for me. They were dedicated people with a sense already pointing to ground realities, because they were really living in it. Talking to them was the beginning of a long integral process of understanding of what architecture should be and what it definitely cannot be.

Piero and Gloria were already engaged in designing and building small projects in the middle of Auroville's nowhere, with local masons, carpenters and materials. There were no structural engineers or contractors

FACING PAGE
At Promesse, 1970: Piero, Gloria and Poppo with their daughter, Grazi

around; nobody could read drawings, let alone mark a building on the ground. For the usual architect, it was a beginning from scratch. Everything had to be improvised on the spot, and that too in Tamil, a different language.

In April 1970, on moving to Auroville, I found myself following in Gloria's and Piero's footsteps, literally. They both shared their work studio with me for three years. They had their projects, as I had mine.

Influences

The first thing that I noticed on joining their studio was a postcard-sized paper stuck on the wall, on which was written in longhand by The Mother a message for the year of 1969 (she would write a message every year): "DON'T TALK – ACT."

Remarkable, I thought. *That's strange*! But since we were already in 1970, was it also meant for me?

Piero gave me the first kickback into structural design. In school, we had learned the basics of it in such a way that we never felt encouraged to do it by ourselves. Instead, we cultivated a high respect, even fear, towards the subject. Structural calculations are done all over the world by engineers. In Auroville, however, none were available. So, the fastest way of proceeding with the design was to do the calculations and drawings oneself.

One of my first jobs was to construct the roof of a shed at Auro Orchard in 1970, designed by Piero and Gloria. I remember marking the building layout on ground with several wooden plugs and nails. Soon, I learned that Indian timber is like iron and the iron-nails, in turn, seem to have some element of butter in

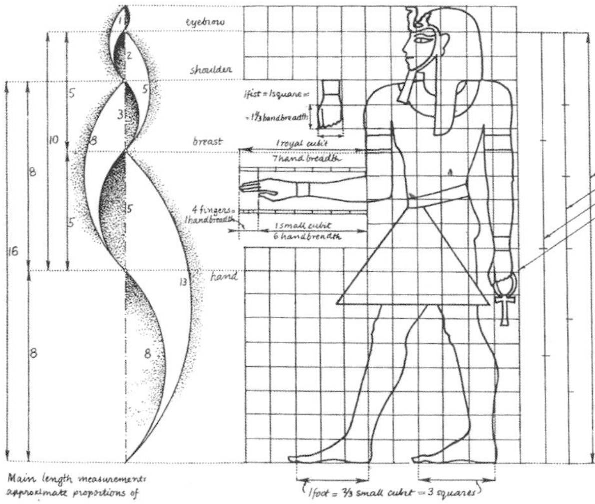

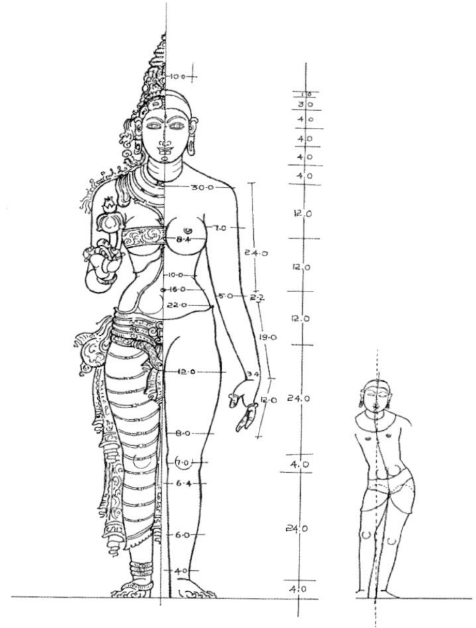

LINEAR MEASUREMENTS OF FEMALE FIGURES BASED ON UTTAMA NAVATALA

LEFT Proportioning system in ancient Egyptian paintings

RIGHT Proportioning system in Indian sculptures still in use today in varied forms of art

FACING PAGE
LEFT The Vitruvian Man by Leonardo da Vinci, 1490

RIGHT The Modular by Le Corbusier, 1948

As all life ought to be sacred, I am reminded that "true art" in built form is one in which the eternal is allowed to breathe and mark its presence, while the mind stays still and speechless. Gurdjieff called this phenomenon "objective architecture". This is more elaborately described or circumscribed with different terminology in Sri Aurobindo's *Foundation of Indian Culture*.

"Indian sacred architecture of whatever date, style or dedication goes back to something timelessly ancient and now outside India almost wholly lost, something which belongs to the past, and yet it goes forward too, though this the rationalistic mind will not easily admit, to something which will return upon us and is already beginning to return, something which belongs to the future. An Indian temple, to whatever godhead it may be built, is in its inmost reality an altar raised to the divine Self, a house of the Cosmic Spirit, an appeal and aspiration to the Infinite."[2]

The Ancients had it; we have lost it.

Contradictory to contemporary interpretations of architecture (as well as all other art forms) that mostly rely on modern trends, fashionable viewpoints and architectural marketing—boosting novelties as human achievements with a lack of historical knowledge and understanding—this presence, in comparison, shines out simply, humbly, noiselessly, demanding much less. It says also that the credit for it goes straight back to its *source*, instead to the ego-ridden architect whose illusion made him or her the sole and only originator of the art.

Piero's and Gloria's sense of beauty lies embedded untold in a simplicity, not a puritan simplicity, metaphorically speaking: of a white bedsheet lying on a white mattress covered by a white bed cover, as to define or coin it as "dhoti architecture", to make it appear sacred or spiritual.

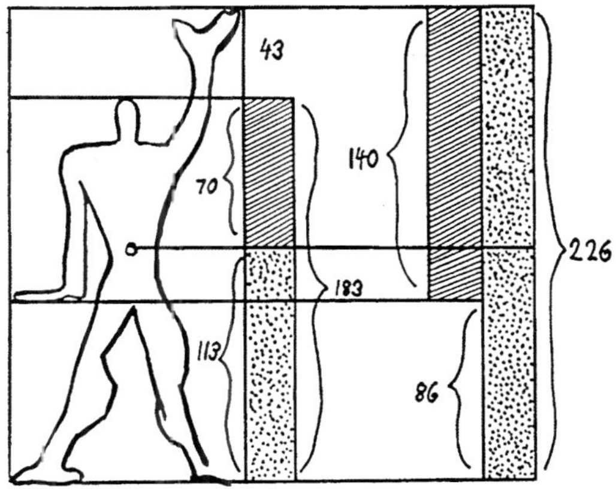

Their work is a play of structural elements—intrinsically related to strength, capacity and gravity—resting on the ground, almost as a child defines it. Beauty appears by itself as almost unwanted or as an incidental consequence. The mastery of details, whichever the materials be chosen—the meeting of the vertical and the horizontal—is proportionately clean with simple junctions. It is perceived simply like a leaf sitting on a twig, all without any intellectual fuss. Black and white, a gift of contrasts given to us by nature, brings their building masses and elements, near and far, into a harmonious dance of shadows and, if not, leaves the white as a canvas for earth colours.

Horizontality is earth's nature, perpendicular to the gravity of the earth. Here and there, their consciousness shines humbly through the unexplainable almost unexpectedly, supported by a dominating, inescapable power of a double or triple horizontality. Was it designed consciously or was it a by-product of a lifelong yoga, which began in a Mars-like barren land for a unique Auroville to evolve, unfolding out of nothing, in spite of turmoil and battles?

This consciousness determines Piero's and Gloria's work, and not the other way around. To cultivate and incorporate this phenomenon of the unexplainable into our work will ultimately be followed by a mastery of forming space in all aspects in future. It will definitely bring with it true art and beauty as the geometry of the silent divine action.

Notes

1. William Blake to Thomas Butts, 22 November 1802 in Letters, 46.
2. *Complete Works of Sri Aurobindo*, Vol. 20, p. 272, Sri Aurobindo Ashram, Pondicherry.

CHRONOLOGY OF WORKS

ITALY 1963-67

Casa della Comunita' di Agape
Prali, Italy, 1958
Piero with Giovanni Koenig

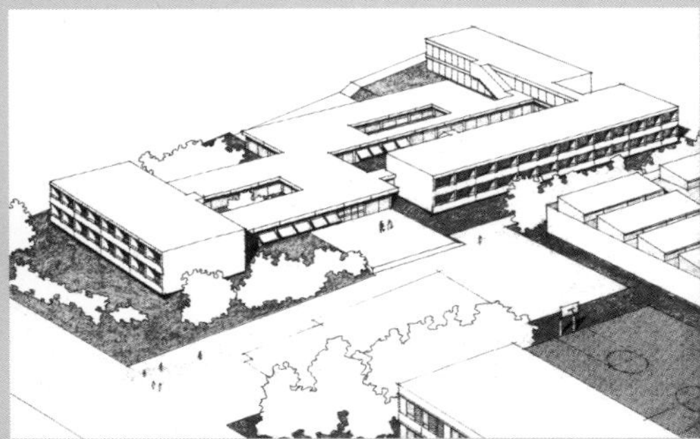

Senior People Home, Racconigi,
Italy, 1963
Piero with Manfredi & Todros

Secondary School, Torino,
Italy, 1963–64
Piero as part of Collettivo di Architettura

House on the Hills, Torino,
Italy, 1965–67
Piero as part of Collettivo di Architettura

Holiday House, Elba Island,
Italy, 1966
Piero and Gloria

Secondary School, Agrigento,
Italy, 1967
Piero as part of Collettivo di Architettura

India 1968-2013

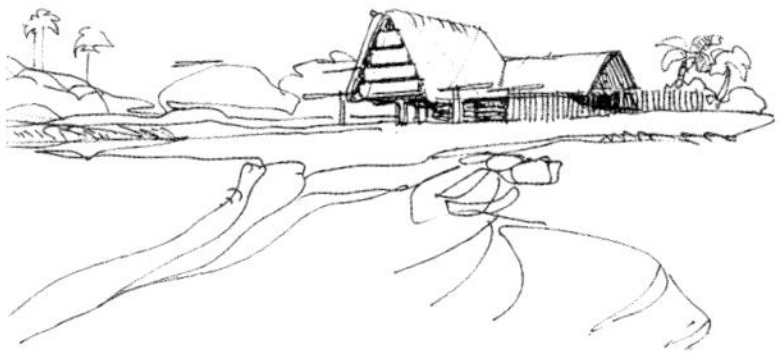

Samarpan beach,
Auroville, 1968

Interiors of Cottage Industry Guest House,
Pondicherry, 1969

Auroson's Home, Certitude,
Auroville, 1969–70

Storeroom for Agricultural Produce, AuroOrchard,
Auroville, 1969–70

1960-1969

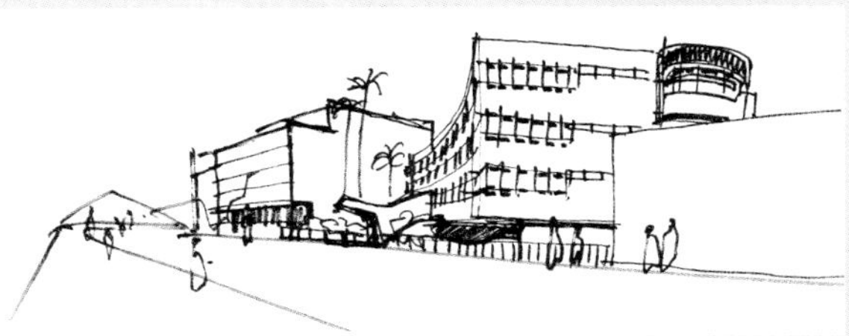

Sri Aurobindo Ashram Nursing Home,
Pondicherry, 1970

Aspiration Community for 80 people,
Auroville, 1969–72

Janet House,
Auroville, 1972

Aspiration Community Kitchen,
Auroville, 1972–74

Matrimandir Excavation & Foundations,
Auroville, 1972–73

1970-1979

1970-1979

Cluster of Three Houses, Certitude,
Auroville, 1972–73

Health Centre, First Phase, Aspiration,
Auroville, 1972–76

Roger Toll House, Certitude,
Auroville, 1973–74

Water Tank, Certitude,
Auroville, 1977

Matrimandir Inner Chamber Structure,
Auroville, 1976-79

Navoditte's House, Certitude,
Auroville, 1977

1980-1989

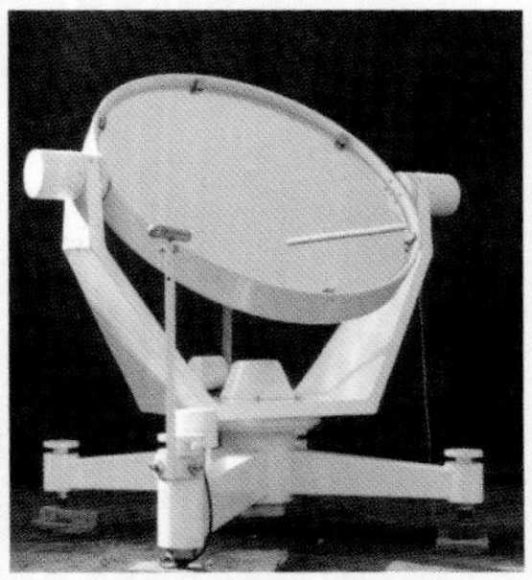

Matrimandir Heliostat,
Auroville, 1981–95

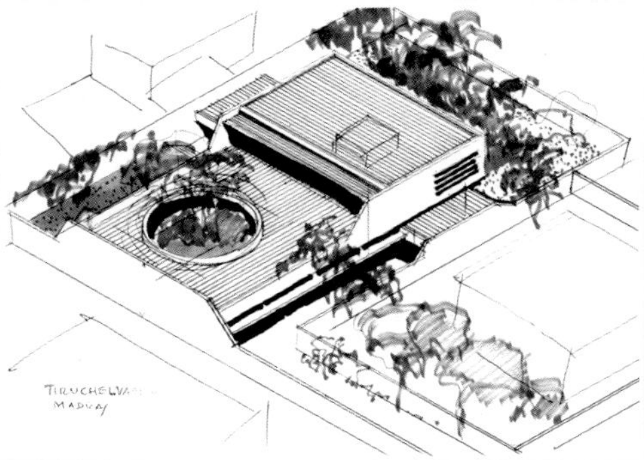

Thiruchelvam House,
Chennai, 1981

Ed and Mauna's House, Forecomers,
Auroville, 1983–84

Matrimandir Ribs,
Auroville, 1974–76

Andy's House, Certitude,
Auroville, 1975

Shyamsunder's House, Certitude,
Auroville, 1975–76

New Community, Certitude,
Auroville, 1977–79

Row Houses, Certitude,
Auroville, 1977–78

Matrimandir Space Frame,
Auroville, 1979–87

Transition School Campus, First Phase,
Auroville, 1985–86

Vivek: Transition School Workshop,
Auroville, 1986–87

Gymnasium dome, Certitude,
Auroville, 1987

Matrimandir Inner Chamber: Interior,
Auroville, 1988–91

1990-1999

Shanti: Transition School Library Building, Auroville, 1990–91

Pierre Charles's House, Dana, Auroville, 1992

Rika's House, Certitude, Auroville, 1992–93

Mitra: Transition School Classrooms, Auroville, 1994–96

Ilse's House, Gaia's Garden, Auroville, 1998

Transition School Classrooms, Auroville, 1999–2004

2000 onwards

Unity Pavillion, International Zone, Auroville, 2001–13

Future School Library Building, Auroville, 2007

Franca's Guest House,
Auroville, 1992

Franca's Studio,
Auroville, 1993

Health Centre, Second Phase, Aspiration,
Auroville, 1994

Future School,
Auroville, 2000–03

Luise House, Verite, Industrial Zone,
Auroville, 2004–06

Transition School Arts & Crafts Building,
Auroville, 2005

Transition Library Building Extension,
Auroville, 2007–09

Shyama's House, Certitude,
Auroville, 2008–09

Unrealized Projects

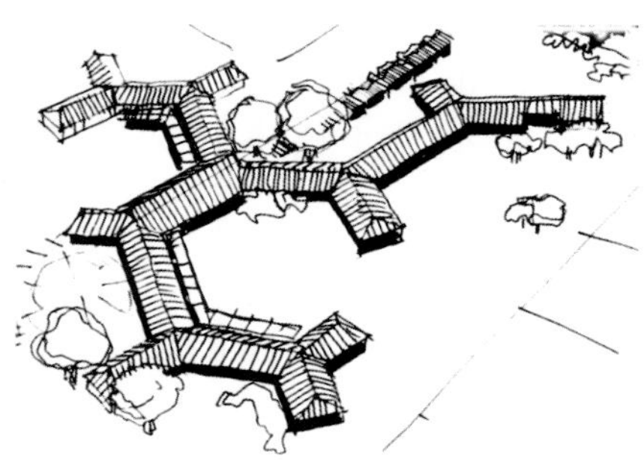

Experimental School,
Auroville, 1968

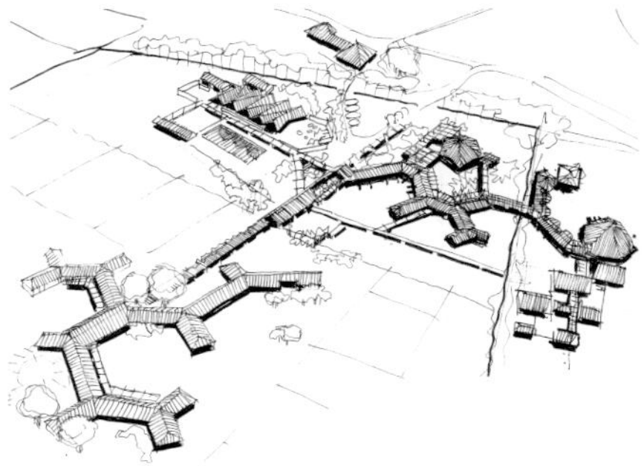

Tibetan Hostel,
Auroville, 1969

Indian Oil Motel and Apartments,
Auroville, 1969

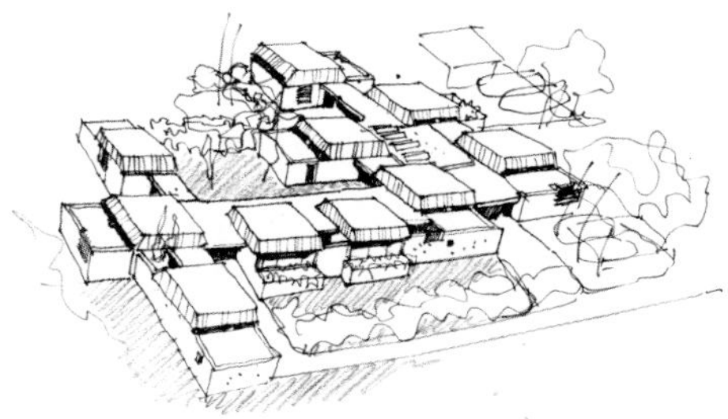

Rural Dispensary,
Pondicherry, 1975

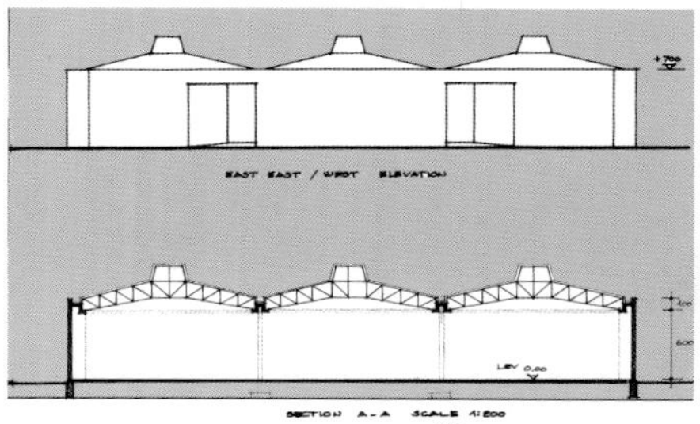

Aurosolvex: Solvent Extraction Plant, **Anegondy,**
Hampi, 1978

Ashram for Sri Aurobindo Disciples,
Hampi, 1978

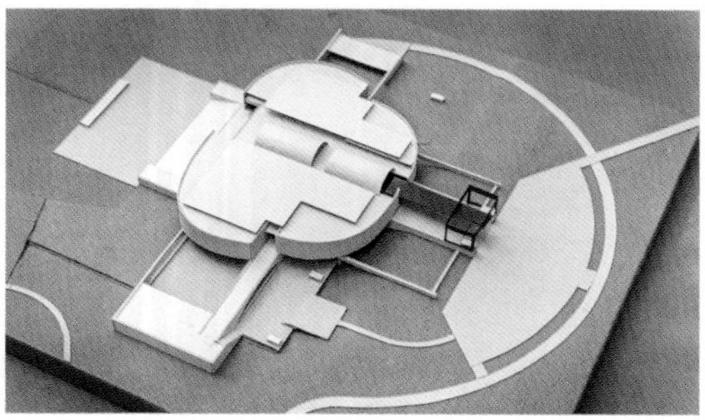

Tagore Art Museum II, **Santiniketan,**
Calcutta, 1985

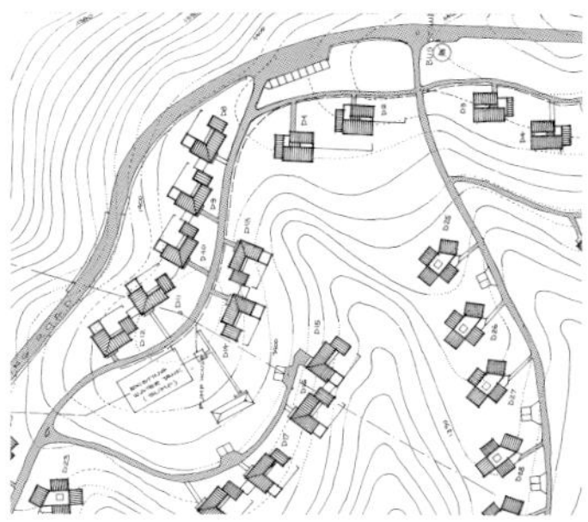

Shillong Housing Project,
Megahalaya, 1987

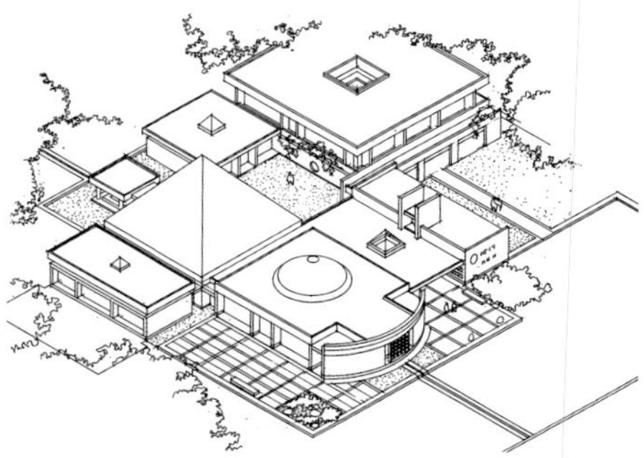

Auroville Meeting Hall, Administrative Zone,
Auroville, 1996

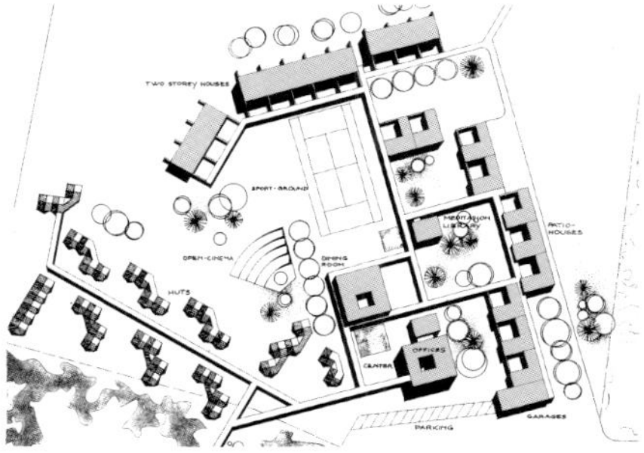

Model Village, Hope,
Auroville, 1969

Service Farm: Housing,
Auroville, 1969–71

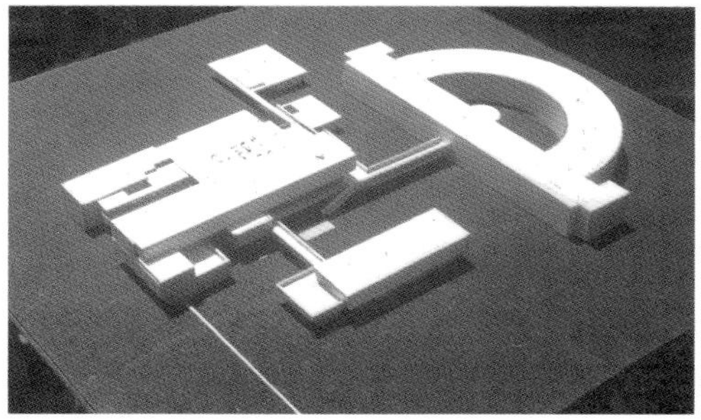

Art School Extension,
Pondicherry, 1970

Samuel's House,
Bangalore, 1984

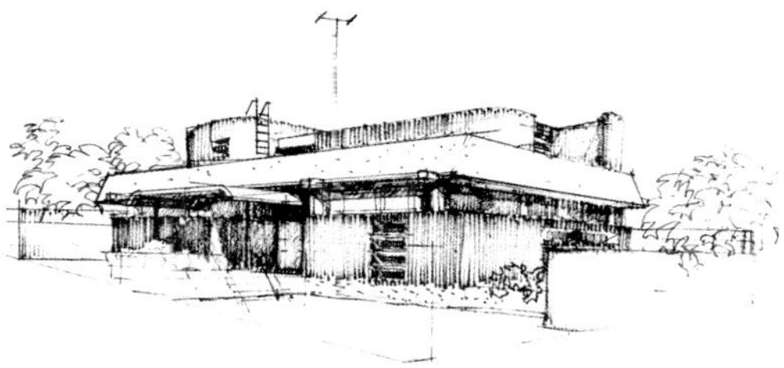

Nigam House,
Lucknow, 1985

Tagore Art Museum I, Santiniketan,
Calcutta, 1985

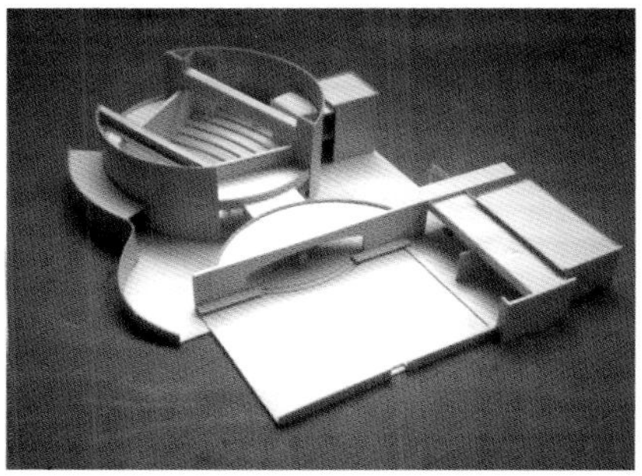

Music Centre II, Cultural Zone,
Auroville, 1998

Auroville Swimming Pool, Cultural Zone,
Auroville, 1999

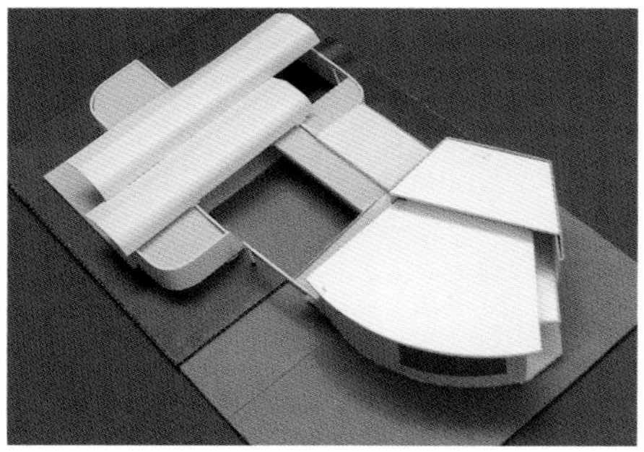

Theatre Workshop, Transition School,
Auroville, 2007

Bibliography

ARCHITECTURE + DESIGN, March–April 1991, 28–39.

Auroville Architecture: Towards new forms for a new consciousness. Auroville, Prisma, 2014 [Fifth edition].

Bhatt, Vikram and Scriver, Peter. *Contemporary Indian Architecture: After the Masters.* Ahmedabad, Mapin Publishing, 1990.

Doctor, Mona. "Form, Structure and Energy—A study of The Great Pyramid and Matrimandir." Unpublished diploma thesis, CEPT University, India, 1990.

Doctor-Pingel, Mona. "Does modern architecture lead to civilization sicknesses?" Unpublished master's thesis. Appropriate Rural Technology and Extension Skills (ARTES), University of Flensburg, Germany, 1994.

Darr, Dominique. *Matrimandir: Hymn to the builder of the future.* Centre d'Art [Art Centre Edition].

Fleig, Karl (co-editor). *Alvar Aalto: Complete works.* Switzerland, Birkhaeuser, 1963 [First edition].

Kundoo, Anupama. *Roger Anger, Research on Beauty.* Germany, Jovis Verlag GmBH, 2009.

Lithman, Alan (Savitra). *Auroville: Sun word rising.* Auroville, Published by Auroville, 1974.

Lithman, Alan (Savitra). *Auroville, The first six years: 1968-1974.* Auroville, Auropublication, 1974.

Lobell, John. *Between Silence and Light – Spirit in the Architecture of Louis I. Kahn.* Boston, Shambhala Publications Inc., 1979.

Architecture of: Asha & Prabhakar Baste, Leo Perreira, Gerard Da Cunha, Kamu Iyer, Sen Kapadia. Monographs Series. Mohile Parikh Centre for the Visual Arts, Architecture Forum. The National Centre for Performing Arts, 1997–2001.

Nakashima, George. *The soul of a tree: A woodworker's reflections.* Tokyo, Kodanshe, 1981.

Frank Lloyd Wright. *Die Meisterwerke.* Kohlahmmaer GmBh, Pfeffier Bruce Books, 1993.

Lubicz, R.A. Schwaller de. *The Temple in Man: Sacred Architecture and The Perfect Man.* Inner Traditions Paperback, 1981.

Shradhavan. *Golconde: A Look behind.* Pondicherry, Mother India, February 1989.

Thomas, Smith Gordon. *Vitruvius on Architecture.* The Monacelli Press, 2003.

"The Auroville Experience." Selections from *Auroville Today* (2006).

The Four Conversations on Matrimandir. *Mother Agenda* (31 December 1969–17 January 1970).

The Mother on Auroville. Pondicherry, Sri Aurobindo Ashram Press, 1999.

"Building the right thing." Interview with Piero by Christine Devin. *Turning Points.* Auroville Press Publisher, 2008.

Ricci, Leonardo. "The Involved Man." *Progressive Architecture* (August 1960).

"A Monterinaldi, Presso Firenze: un centro di quindici case, di Leonardo Ricci, arch." *Domus* [Italian Edition] (December 1957).

Egeraat, Corinne van. *Dislocated for the Love of Architecture.* 4 April 2009. "Dislocated," An online documentary project for the broadcaster HUMAN (2009/2010).

Syril, Schochen. "A movement is abroad: An Aurovilian's journey towards the City of Dawn." Journal of the Integral Yoga of Sri Aurobindo and The Mother [Collaboration] 32 (Summer 2007).

Websites

www.auroville.org

www.sriaurobindosashram.org

www.creativecommons.org

Documentary Sources

Gautier, Francois and Rakhal. "Gloria: Serving the Construction of Matrimandir." Yatra Multimedia Auroville, 2013.

Gautier, Francois and Rakhal. "The Matrimandir: Honouring Piero Ciconesi." Yatra Multimedia Auroville, 2015.

Kalker, Doris Van and Francis Neemberry. "Building Matrimandir: Labour of Love." Video Documentary. Auroville Video Production, 2008.

Photographs and Illustrations Credits

Peter Anderschitz: p. 10.

Auroville Archives: pp. 11, 23 r, 58, 63 a-l & a-r, 73 a, 77 b, 81 b, 84 l & r-b, 94 l, 120 r, 148 a-l, 148 b, 149 b-l, 155 a, 156 b, 191 (first row: l).

Auroville Archives / Mirao Pingel: p. 18.

Auroville Archives / Paolo Tommasi: p. 62 l.

Auroville Archives / PRISMA: pp. 16–17, 120 r.

Auroville Archives / Roger Anger: pp. 62 r, 76 a-r, 114 a.

Gloria Cicionesi: pp. 40, 44 b.

Grazi Cicionesi: p. 204.

Piero Cicionesi: pp. 26, 39 l, 47 a & b, 67 l, 78 b, 83, 90 a-l, 91 a, 121 b-l, 124 a-r & b, 129 b, 132 r-a & r-b, 133 b, 137 a-l, 138, 139 l, 140 a & b, 141 b, 144 b, 151 a-l, b-l & b-r, 154 l & r, 156 a, 157 a-l & b-l, 158 l-a & l-b, 159, 161 a & c-l & c-r, 162 a-l & a-r, 169 a, 172 b-l, 173 l-a & r, 178 a, 185 a & b, 190 (first row: l & r; second row: l, c & r), 191 (third row: l), 192 (first row: c; second row: l, c & r; third row: l & r), 193 (first row: c & r; second row: c; third row: l, c-l & c-r), 194 (first row: l & c; second row: l & c), 195 (first row: l, c & r; second row: r), 196 (first row: r; third row: l), 197 (first row: c & r; second row: r; third row: l, c & r).

Dominique Darr: pp. 12, 23 l, 24, 59, 65 a & b, 69 a, 70, 72 l, 82 a, 94 r, 95, 107 a-r, 107 b, 109 a, b-l & b-r, 110 a, 111, 116 r, 120 l, 121 a, 121 b-r, 125, 149 a, 153 b, 183, 191 (second row: c), 192 (first row: l).

Mona Doctor-Pingel: p. 137 a-r.

Domus/Casali: pp. 42 a, 43 r, 100, 134 b-r.

Franz Fassbender: pp. 123 r-a, 134 a, 136.

Ereno Guerci: p. 173 l-b.

Andre Hababou: p. 74 l.

Brigitte Jacob: p. 39 r.

Erik Kråkström: p. 46 l & r.

John Mandeen: pp. 79, 80 l, 88, 96, 101, 103, 171 b, 174–175, 177 a, 181 a, 193 (second row: r).

Pino Marchese: p. 53 a & b.

Giorgio Molinari: pp. 60–61, 75, 85, 92 r, 93, 97, 116 l, 123 l, 124 a-l, 128 b, 135 a, 164 a, 165 a, 166 r, 167, 170 a, 172 a-r, 176 a & b, 180 a & b, 181 b, 193 (third row: r), 194 (second row: r; third row: r), 195 (second row: l; third row: l).

Matrimandir Archives: pp. 68, 69 b, 72 r, 73 b, 77 a, 78 a, 82 b, 84 r-a, 87 b, 89 a, 92 l.

Matrimandir Archives / Surya: pp. 87 a, 89 b, 90 a-r & b, 102.

Shiraz Panthaki: pp. 22 b, 112–113, 115 r, 117, 118 b, 126–127, 127, 130, 142, 143, 144 a, 145, 191 (first row: c-r), 195 (second row: c).

Poppo Pingel: pp. 184 b, 191 (first row: r).

Indra Poddar: p. 184 a.

PRISMA: pp. 19 a, 49 l-b, 98, 149 b-r, 192 (first row: r), 194 (first row: r).

Progressive Architecture 1960: p. 43 l.

Niharika Sanyal: pp. 115 l, 134 b-l, 157 b-r, 170 b-r, 171 a, 172 b-r, 177 b, 194 (third row: l), 195 (third row: r).

Sri Aurobindo Ashram Archives: pp. 19 b, 49 l-a.

Barun Tagore: pp. 49 l-b, 107 a-l.

Wikimedia Commons: pp. 32 a, 33 l, 41 a-r, 45 a & b, 52 b, 187 l.

www.abitare.it: p. 42 b.

www.auroville.org: pp. 191 (third row: r), 193 (first row: l).

www.flickr.com: pp. 22 a, 31 a, 32 b, 41 b.

Architectural drawings, illustrations and models by Piero Cicionesi unless otherwise noted.

Best efforts have been made to obtain permission for:

Giovanni Michelucci, 1960 (p. 52)

Proportioning system in ancient Egyptian paintings, reproduced from *The Temple of Man* by R. A. Schwaller de Lubicz (p. 186 l).

Proportioning system in Indian sculptures, reproduced from *Indian Sculpture and Iconography* by V Ganapati Sthapati (p. 186 r).

The Modular by Le Corbusier (p. 187 r).

[Numbers refer to page numbers]

[a=above, b=below, l=left, c=centre, r=right, a-l=above left, a-r=above right, b-l=below left, b-r=below right, c-l=centre-left, c-r=centre-right, l-a=left-above, l-b=left-below, r-a=right-above, r-b=right-below]

Contributors

Dr Chamanlal Gupta

Dr Chamanlal Gupta is a highly reputed building physicist, both nationally and internationally, in the field of solar energy. He lives in Sri Aurobindo Ashram, Pondicherry, since 1967. He has been mentoring students and researchers/practitioners, in the fields of solar energy, biogas technology and green building practices, for more than five decades. Since 1971, he has been in several renewable energy committees of the Government of India and is currently teaching at the Sri Aurobindo International Centre of Education at Pondicherry.

Pino Marchese

Pino Marchese studied architecture at the University of Florence (1990) and has been running an independent practice in Auroville since 1998. He believes in a holistic approach to design involving functionality, aesthetics and resource conservation. Design for him is a search for timeless architecture that is beyond trends and doesn't struggle to be new or inventive simply for the sake of it.

Poppo Pingel

Poppo Pingel came to Auroville in 1970 from Germany and has since been involved in designing and building projects in and around Auroville. Highly personal and Zen-like in his approach, Poppo is known for buildings that respond to the climate, landscape and culture of the place. A complete oeuvre of his works has been published as a monograph under the Auroville Architects Monograph Series written by Mona Doctor-Pingel and published by Mapin in 2012.

Niharika Sanyal

Niharika Sanyal learned a little bit about unlearning while at CEPT University, Ahmedabad. Following her research into how to humanize prison architecture, she became fascinated by how the pursuit of meaning through creativity can lead to human flourishing. This, coupled with pursuits in writing, experiences in teaching children and a stint in Auroville, has led her towards the study of human psychology.

Poonam Verma Mascarenhas

Poonam Verma Mascarenhas is an architect, conservationist, researcher and writer, with keen interest in contextual architecture. Inherent wisdom of traditional building designs and technologies have engaged her for more than two decades and contemporising the same is the cornerstone of her Goa-based, award-winning studio Archinova Environs. She is the author of *Kerala Heritage Guide* (2000) listing six districts of Kerala, *Silent Sentinels: Traditional Architecture of Coorg* (2005) and she has also contributed to the monograph on architect Poppo Pingel (Mapin, 2012).

Sketch of Piazza del Mercato in Siena, ink and watercolour, by Piero Cicionesi, 1958

ACKNOWLEDGEMENTS

I would like to put on record my deep gratitude to Piero and Gloria for their patience during the many interviews and questioning of their life and work. My curiosity and the ever-changing team working on the analysis, layouts and graphics with enthusiastic energy must have surely tested their endurance. They were very reticent and even unfamiliar with putting their thoughts to words, being used to internalize and not externalize their creative decision-making process or to talk of their struggles within the community over the years. But slowly, they have extracted out of their deep caverns some amazing insights, photos and sketches that have left me humbled and in awe of their gifted skills, humility and determination.

Poonam Verma Mascarenhas of Archinova Environs, Goa has been a strong support and an honest sounding board. On each of her visits to Auroville in the past five years, we spent days brainstorming, poring over years of collected material. She helped give final shape to this book with her critical inputs. Niharika Sanyal, a young architect from CEPT University, Ahmedabad, who trained at my studio in 2012, came back to work untiringly and quietly giving final shape to this book. On her two visits to Auroville for this monograph, she helped to analyse, archive and finally to work on the complete layout proposal for Mapin. She has been a pleasure to work with.

Many others have contributed to making this work possible. I would like to particularly thank Tushita Gandhi for research assistance, patient archiving, scanning, transcription and initial graphics; Durganand Balsavar, for his engagement and valuable critical inputs; Chandana Reddy and Eleanor Figueiredo, who worked in my studio to help organize the manuscript and layouts; Gilles Guigan of Auroville Archives, for his passion to research the history of Auroville and generously share it at any time.

For the photos published in this book, I would like to thank the late Dominique Darr for her hospitality in France in 2007 and for sharing her entire archives for my research; and Francine Finck, who continues the work of archiving Darr's huge collection at Centre d'Art, Citadine, Auroville. Thanks are also due to John Mandeen, Shiraz Panthaki and Giorgio Molinari for making available their beautifully shot photos over many years, sometimes shooting specific angles on request. I troubled many Aurovilians for their time and memories regarding Piero and Gloria. In particular, I thank Frederick Shulze-Buxloh,

Shyama, Auroson and Andy Martens for their interviews. Special thanks also to Grazi and Marta Cicionesi for their support and work on the photographs. Architect Anupama Kundoo and I were co-authoring this series initially, and I acknowledge her contribution in those early stages.

This idea of writing comprehensive monographs on Auroville architects could only take concrete shape due to a research grant made available through the Project Coordination Group of Auroville from Stichting de Zaaier, Netherlands, in 2006. I am also grateful to Prof. Vijay Sohoni, past president of Indian Council of Architecture, for giving a research grant in 2010 and Jayashree Deshpande, Director, Council of Architecture Training and Research Centre (COA-TRC), for supporting this work and recognizing the valuable contribution of Auroville architects to India.

I thank Bipin Shah of Mapin Publishing, who extended his support once again in publishing the second book in this series, and to his very helpful staff at Ahmedabad, in particular, Gopal Limbad, Rakesh Manger, Neha Manke, Ateendriya Gupta and Sarayu Narasimhan.

I would like to thank my mother, Vanlila Doctor, who has always been an anchor and a source of strength in my life, as well as my late father, Ramakant Bhailal Doctor, who instilled a sense of freedom and idealism in me. Last but not the least, I thank Poppo, my husband and friend, who never forgot to ask patiently about the status of this monograph in the past five years, supporting me to finish what I aspired to do!

Mona Doctor-Pingel,
November 2017

The author Mona Doctor-Pingel
in discussion with Piero and
Gloria Cicionesi, 2017